PRAISE FOR
*WE CAN SEE INTO ANOTHER PLACE:
MILE-HIGH WRITERS ON SOCIAL JUSTICE*

"This book is lovely, instructive, thought-provoking, and occasionally hard to read for all the right reasons. These stories, poems, plays, and graphic artwork are deeply important. Study these works, and you can learn an enormous amount of beneficial knowledge. I also loved the introductory essay and the questions at the end about how to create the best possible future we can make going forward."

–HELEN THORPE, author of *The Newcomers, Soldier Girls* and *Just Like Us*

"*We Can See into Another Place: Mile-High Writers on Social Justice* offers readers a rare opportunity: the chance to hear from a broad, inclusive group of storytellers using varied creative forms. Through these works, we discover how our humanity unites us. That is the power of outstanding creative work—and outstanding creative work is in abundance in this collection."

–CYNTHIA SWANSON, *New York Times* bestselling author of *The Bookseller* and *The Glass Forest*; editor of *Denver Noir*

"*We Can See into Another Place* settles in the harmony of a vast array of unexpectedly intertwined voices. Its nimble interplay of genres and formats confirms the space we can hold for endless shapes, visions, and possibilities."

–VINIYANKA PRASAD, co-executive director & founder, The Word | A Storytelling Sanctuary

T0282014

"*We Can See into Another Place* is an extraordinary volume of literary work that spans the arc of genres…the caliber of writing drew me in so I sat down and spent the next two days reading…open the cover and begin and you'll be conscience of your perspectives on the world and society and people changing, giving you a sharper, deeper wisdom and greater love for being alive. This book challenges you to change, to grow, to embrace the other.…A treasure for all of us."

–JIMMY SANTIAGO BACA, author of *A Place to Stand* and *No Enemies*

We Can See into Another Place

We Can See into Another Place

MILE-HIGH WRITERS
ON SOCIAL JUSTICE

EDITED BY ANDREA REXILIUS

WITH OLIVIA ABTAHI · R. ALAN BROOKS · STEVEN DUNN · CAROLINA EBEID
STEVEN COLE HUGHES · KRISTEN IVERSEN · TRACI L. JONES · TARASHEA NESBIT
LORI OSTLUND · KHADIJAH QUEEN · JENNY SHANK · SUZI Q. SMITH
CHRISTINE SNEED · MATHANGI SUBRAMANIAN · ADDIE TSAI · DENISE VEGA
RACHEL WEAVER · DAVID HESKA WANBLI WEIDEN · ERIKA T. WURTH

THE
BOOKIES
PRESS

BOWER
HOUSE

DENVER

Edited by Heather Garbo, Evelyn Hampton and Andrea Rexilius
Design and cover art by HR Hegnauer
Printed in Canada

Library of Congress Control Number: 2024937479

Paperback: ISBN 978-1-917895-21-7
Ebook: ISBN 978-1-917895-22-4

10 9 8 7 6 5 4 3 2 1

CONTENTS

PART I: Voice

PART II: Body

PART III: Landscapes

PART IV: Futures

"I dwell in Possibility."

—EMILY DICKINSON

Introduction

"In the dark times
Will there also be singing?
Yes, there will also be singing
About the dark times."
—BERTOLT BRECHT, motto to *Svendborg Poems*, 1939

In curating the pieces for this anthology, I thought of Audre Lorde's words, "I am deliberate / and afraid / of nothing," because being deliberate, living a life of purposeful examination and reflection on the conditions and manufactured realities around us, is exactly the kind of work writers and academics should be doing. And being "afraid / of nothing," including the dismantling of one's own mind from within the larger power structures, institutions being one of those, is to take a leap of faith toward an unknown future.

Allowing that future to be hopeful, full of possibility, while also rooted in uncertainty, is the kind of fearlessness writers are deeply capable of performing. Writers, after all, are the fools of society, the ones who pursue their goals despite the odds in a capitalistic system, the ones who believe the voices of the many are valuable with or without monetary gain, who seek insight, growth, change, and vulnerability, who understand the nature of storytelling and its relationship to our social, cultural, economic, racial, and gendered realities. It is the writer who can weave a new story, a new way of relating and being in the world.

We Can See into Another Place is an anthology featuring writers and faculty from the low-residency Mile-High MFA in Creative Writing Program in Denver, Colorado, that examines inequity while keeping an ever-growing light burning in the face of that strife, one that glows toward the possibility of newly imagined futures, futures that encourage empathy, compassion, and the fight toward a more just society. Emily Dickinson writes, "If your nerve deny you— / go above your nerve." Often it is this act of going "above your nerve" that allows the most poignant stories, essays, and poems to find their way to the page, to give voices, bodies, landscapes, and futures maps toward visibility and re-envisioned pathways of hope.

PART I: *Voice*

The anthology opens with a section on "voice" that examines the various ways in which voices are silenced, via gun violence (in R. Alan Brooks' "A Tragedy in the Snow"), via cultural genocide (in David Heska Wanbli Weiden's "Carlisle Longings), via political oppression and book banning (in Steven Cole Hughes's "A Brief History of Banned Books"), via domestic violence and abuse (in Addie Tsai's "Writing as a Vessel for Chaos: A Letter to High Schoolers"), via the indelible pierce of warfare and grief (in Carolina Ebeid's series of "Punctum" poems), and via white supremacist notions of language (in Steven Dunn's "Intro / An Excerpt from *Travel with Nas*"). Throughout each of these pieces a notion of reclamation, through compassion, historical research, humor, self-expression, revolt, and self-education, is threaded. In his graphic narrative piece, R. Alan Brooks asks, "In the face of such tragedy, can art be something worthwhile?" This question is beautifully answered by Brooks himself: "There's a reason dictators & politicians ban your art. It's because they have no doubts about its power," as well as by each individual author's text in this section on voice and the restorative power of language to see into another place.

PART II: *Body*

Part II, "Body," moves us through various time periods and contexts into an intimate look at the lives of young women and the ways in which they are often reduced to mere bodies without any agency of their own. Moving through cultural moments of gendered violence, women's rights, and LGBTQIA+ experiences, the pieces in this section provide a vigil as well as a powerful attempt to reconcile our pasts (and futures) by providing female and queer bodies a space to fight back, to tell their stories with a renewed sense of agency and understanding that the crimes against them (their bodies and beings) are not shames they should endure, but harms that require imminent correction. As Mathangi Subramanian writes, "These days, other people's mistakes are just too heavy to hold."

PART III: *Landscapes*

The section on "landscapes" considers our relationship to place, whether that place be neurological or relational, rooted in an apocalyptic landscape or in our relationships to home, family, self, or environment. This section opens with a poem by Khadijah Queen that asks us to "Remember / when pain was not to be seen or looked at, / but institutionalized. Invisible, unspoken, / transformed but not really transformed." Jenny Shank and Rachel Weaver take us to places of neurological transformation. And Christine Sneed and TaraShea Nesbit traverse realms of home and family. This section concludes with an experimental poetic play by Queen, "The Dream Act," which lyrically and surrealistically explores "race, age, gender, and other appearance markers" through the playful deconstruction of stereotyped characters.

PART IV: *Futures*

In this final section of the anthology, we pick up themes of how writing helps us grow into ourselves and provides a sense of discovery and hope for the future. This section ends with an interview with three young adult fiction writers reflecting on the impact of social justice on their work and how they engage with audiences. Finally, we open the act of reflection and sense of discovery to our readers by providing a few questions, and writing space if you're so inclined, to jot down your own notes, ideas, and emotions in relation to some of the topics in this collection. We invite you to continue to consider these questions and your own thoughts on social justice within your communities and ask you to reflect on the ways in which writing and reading has changed your life and your sense of hope for the future.

—ANDREA REXILIUS

Editor's Note: Some of the pieces in this collection contain content that may be distressing to some readers, including but not limited to depictions of violence, and references to child abuse, sexual assault and abortion. Readers who may be sensitive to these elements, please take note.

"Don't let anybody, anybody convince you this
is the way the world is and therefore must be.
It must be the way it ought to be."

   —TONI MORRISON

                    •   •   •

"Though we tremble before uncertain futures
may we meet illness, death and adversity with strength
may we dance in the face of our fears."

   —GLORIA ANZALDÚA

PART I

Voice

R. ALAN BROOKS

A Tragedy in the Snow

WAYNE MURDERED A **TEACHER**--

--WHO WAS HIT BY A BULLET THAT BLASTED THROUGH HIS **CAR** AS HE WAS LEAVING CAMPUS.

WAYNE MURDERED A FELLOW **STUDENT**, WHO'D HEARD THE CAR **CRASH**, AND WALKED OUT OF THE LIBRARY TO **HELP**.

HE INJURED **FOUR MORE**:

A **SECURITY** GUARD--

--AND SEVERAL **OTHER** STUDENTS.

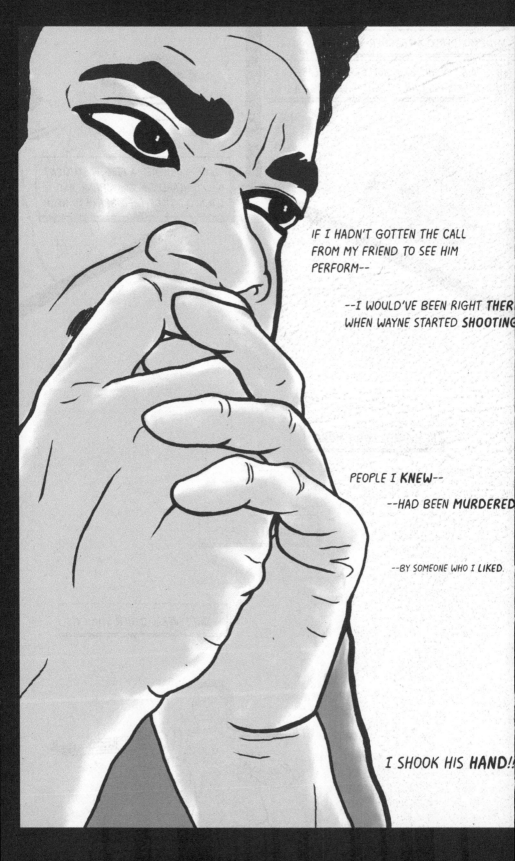

THAT WAS ALMOST **30 YEARS** AGO.

WAYNE HAS SPENT THOSE 3 DECADES IN **PRISON**.

I STILL HAVE NO IDEA **WHY** HE MURDERED THOSE PEOPLE.

I'VE READ HIS EXPLANATIONS IN NEWSPAPERS, AND THEY MAKE NO **SENSE**.

BACK THEN, I THOUGHT, SINCE MY LIFE WAS SOMEHOW **SPARED**--

--IT MUST'VE MEANT THAT I HAD TO DO
SOMETHING **IMPORTANT** WITH MY LIFE--

--TO SOMEHOW **HONOR** THE PEOPLE
WHO WERE **MURDERED** BY WAYNE.

BUT, WHAT?

BUT, WHAT?

BUT...

WHAT?

NOW, AS A GROWN MAN, I THINK ABOUT ALL OF THE QUESTIONS THAT I HAD BACK THEN.
"HOW CAN I CHANGE THE WORLD WITH ART?"
"WHAT CAN I CREATE THAT WILL IMPROVE PEOPLE'S LIVES?"
"IN THE FACE OF SUCH TRAGEDY--
--CAN ART BE SOMETHING WORTHWHILE?"
"OR, IS IT JUST FOOLISH?"
FOR A LONG TIME, I WASN'T SURE.
BUT NOW, I KNOW.
THERE'S A REASON DICTATORS & POLITICIANS BAN YOUR ART.
IT'S BECAUSE THEY HAVE NO DOUBTS ABOUT ITS POWER.
AND IF YOUR ART IS POWERFUL ENOUGH TO SCARE DICTATORS--
--THEN WHY ARE YOU DOUBTING IT?
R. ALAN BROOKS

DAVID HESKA WANBLI WEIDEN

Carlisle Longings

"She often longs for 'Old Carlisle.'"

These are the words that haunt me, the words of my long-dead grandmother.

These are the words that I've kept hidden since I discovered them years ago, telling no one, because they destroy the narrative I've told myself and others.

These are the words where she reveals that she *liked* the Native American boarding school she attended, the notorious Carlisle Indian Industrial School, the first and most hated of the boarding schools. The institutions where Native children were taken after being abducted and separated from their parents. The institutions where the children were robbed of their language, their culture, their spirituality. The places where they were sometimes physically and sexually abused, the places where they too often died, buried in the sad cemeteries on the grounds, their parents not informed until much later. Natives have known the pain of involuntary child separation for generations, long before this became official policy for undocumented immigrant families seeking a better life across the border.

My grandmother liked it there. I know this because she sent an alumna note to the school: "Marie Beauvais writes from Cantonment, Oklahoma, that she is perfectly delighted with her work and surroundings, but that she often longs for 'Old Carlisle.'"

Let me back up here. My maternal grandmother, Marie Beauvais Cordry, was a member of the Rosebud Sioux Tribe—known as the Sicangu Nation in Lakota—on the Rosebud Indian Reservation in South Dakota. She was born October 23, 1890, just two months before the Wounded Knee massacre at the neighboring Pine Ridge Indian Reservation. So she was born almost exactly at the turning point for American Indians in the United States, that final heartbreaking moment when the last bands of resistant Indians were defeated by American soldiers and forced to move to reservations, which were really prison camps at that time. Most historians view the Wounded Knee massacre, which occurred on December 29, 1890, as the end of an era for Natives, the moment when one way of life ended and another began. Being born at that moment, my grandmother only knew life on the reservation, but it's almost certain that she heard considerable lamentations from elders for the customs and traditions that had become a thing of the past, almost in the blink of an eye.

She died when I was very young, so I don't have any real memories of her beyond a few hazy images. Perhaps my strongest memory is of her funeral, where I remember the sadness of my mother and aunties, and that I placed my silver dollar—an unimaginably large sum for a six-year-old back then—into her casket before she was lowered into the ground, wanting to give her something to take with her to the spirit world.

Now, as a middle-aged professor of Native American Studies, I have so many questions I wish I could ask her—family questions, historical questions, personal questions. But I'm forced to piece together what scraps of information I can from the slender official record and from my older cousins who have better, more robust memories. My cousin James tells me that his most vivid memory is of her silently pumping water outside of her house so that she and her grandkids would have something to drink. He tells me that she'd be completely focused on her task—no speaking with the children running about, no hugs, no stories. Just trying to get enough water to survive before the weather turned bitter.

It's distressing to realize that many homes on the reservation still don't have adequate water today, decades after her death. I visit the rez two or three times a year to see family, take part in spiritual ceremonies, and get away from the clamor of the city. When I go there, I always make a pilgrimage to the ruins of her final domicile, a hundred-foot-square shack with no electricity, no running water, and no indoor plumbing. This miserable structure was where she spent the last years of her life, a woman in her late seventies, gathering firewood to stave off the brutal South Dakota winters, trudging out into the woods to make her ablutions, gathering what food she could in the wild and dependent upon family members for sustenance when she couldn't. The shack now lies in pieces, the wooden boards and planks rotting on the ground, no one caring enough to cart them away. I'm filled with anger whenever I visit, as I can't understand why none of her grown children agreed to take her in and instead left her to her own devices in this primitive shack. My mother and all my aunts and uncles are gone, so I'm left with no answers and no one to ask, only a hazy feeling of resentment toward my family for their abandonment of my grandmother.

From the official records I obtained from the National Archives years ago, I know that my grandmother was born at Rosebud to Benjamin and Amy Beauvais, and that she had eight brothers and sisters, two of whom died, ostensibly from "rheumatism" and "brain fever," and that her father was dead at the time of her matriculation at Carlisle. Life for her own mother, Amy Beauvais, must have been hard after living through the death of her husband and two children as well as having six living children to support at a time when traditional Lakota lifeways had been wiped out by the US government. Natives were forced to rely upon the meager rations shipped to the reservations and frequently sold to outsiders by corrupt agents. The official records tell me that Marie Beauvais attended the White Thunder Day School in Wood, South Dakota, from ages nine to fifteen, then one year of school at the St. Francis Indian School, and possibly one year at another Indian school in Chamberlain, South Dakota, although the records are not clear. Then she traveled to Carlisle.

I wonder what it must have been like for her, that trip to Pennsylvania, her first time leaving South Dakota, taking a train across the rolling hills of the Midwest, being joined by other Indians, some younger, some older, all of them going to the school about which they'd almost certainly heard terrible rumors and stories, but perhaps also some positive accounts about the institution and the students there.

What is clear is that she traveled across the country and arrived at the Carlisle Indian School on September 16, 1910, when she was twenty years old. This was not unusual at the time, as many students somewhat older than traditional school ages would enroll at the boarding school for a variety of reasons, usually poverty or the death of a parent. Younger students, however, were often taken to the boarding schools through coercion or force, especially in the early years of the institutions. Government authorities would withhold rations, annuities, and other necessities unless parents agreed to send their children. If the parents continued to resist, state officials would seize the children. The historical literature is replete with references to the drills that Native families practiced, where young children would sprint for the woods when alerted by their parents that the government officers had arrived. It is difficult to imagine the pain these parents must have felt to have their children—some as young as five or six—ripped from their grasps and taken away without any idea of when they would see them again.

But that wasn't the case with my grandmother. The available records suggest that she was not taken by force to Carlisle, but went voluntarily. Voluntarily, that is, if you consider privation and poverty as creating a set of voluntary choices. Marie had been shipped from school to school in South Dakota, almost certainly because her own mother couldn't adequately provide for her and the other five children after the death of their father. Remember that Indians were not always allowed to leave the borders of reservations back then, and there were no jobs, of course. The US government had pursued a policy of extermination of the buffalo, so there was no hunting, even if they had been allowed to leave. The people were forced into a position of dependency where they had to rely upon the goods provided by the government and the almost total authority wielded by the reservation agent. This power tended to encourage corruption by the local officials, and they would withhold food and other items from Indians who were deemed to be too vocal or rebellious. Little wonder, then, that alcohol sometimes became a problem later for the proud people who'd been forced into this miserable existence.

When my grandmother arrived at Carlisle, she received a physical examination by a doctor, who noted that she was 5'8½" tall, weighed 153 pounds, and was in good health. How did she feel when she arrived at the school? Was she excited to be among Indians from hundreds of different nations, or was she apprehensive about the harsh disciplinary practices she'd soon encounter?

I'm constantly surprised by the number of people who aren't aware of this disgraceful episode in our history. Some scholars estimate that, in the period of the late nineteenth and early twentieth centuries, as many as 30 percent of all Native children were separated from their families and taken to off-reservation boarding schools. If Indian day schools and reservation boarding schools are included, then the numbers indicate that over 80 percent of Native children were educated using these methods. The professed objective was to assimilate Indian children into American society, but most scholars agree that the true purpose was cultural genocide. Perhaps it is not surprising that this shameful period is ignored in nearly all primary and secondary education today, given that it goes against the story that we tell ourselves as Americans, the story that says we love freedom and value children.

Nearly every indigenous parent who's raising a child away from traditional lands is aware of the difficulty in reconciling what's being taught in schools with the reality of being Native. I recall my younger son, Sasha, then in second grade, asking me one day about Christopher

Columbus. His teacher had told him that Columbus brought indigenous people back to Spain from the Americas because he liked them and wanted to help them. I'd hesitated, wondering if I should explain that Columbus actually sent a contingent of Natives back to Europe to serve as slaves. Then I considered whether I should talk to Sasha's teacher and try to convince her to change her whitewashed view of American history and adopt a more historically accurate perspective.

But I took the easy way out, deciding to avoid putting a target on my child. I told myself I was doing the right thing, that I'd tell him the truth at home, that his social standing at school was important. When I told this story later to a Native friend, she called me a coward. Although I bristled at her insult, I realized she was right. I'd made one of those countless accommodations every parent of color makes, but at what cost? And of course, the compromises I've had to make for my children pale in comparison to the truly terrible choices faced by Native parents back in the boarding-school days.

In 1885, Commissioner of Indian Affairs Hiram Price stated, "It is cheaper to give them education than to fight them." He was referring to what was known as the "Indian problem." The problem, of course, was what to do with all of the Natives who inconveniently refused to vanish and remained as a living and breathing reminder of the massive injustice that had been committed on a continental scale. Millions of Indians had succumbed to disease, and millions more had been killed in wars, but hundreds of thousands remained in the late 1800s, even though most Americans had never laid eyes on a real Native.

The famous slogan from that time was, "Kill the Indian to save the man." This was Captain Richard Henry Pratt's guiding philosophy for the creation of the Carlisle Industrial Indian School. Pratt used his experience educating Native prisoners using a military-style form of education to convince Congress to grant him the use of an abandoned Army barracks in Carlisle, Pennsylvania, to found the first off-reservation Native boarding school. He equated indigeneity with ignorance, poverty, and immorality, and he was firmly convinced that Native Americans required only the introduction of "civilizing" practices to convert them to the capitalistic ways of the new nation. Pratt believed that inculcation into Western values would convert backward Indians—who believed in communal ownership of property and the sharing of wealth—into hardworking capitalists. William Torrey Harris, later the US Commissioner of Education, summarized these principles at the 1883 Lake Mohonk Conference on Indian Affairs; the quotation comes from the book *Education for Extinction* by David Wallace Adams:

> [A]ttributes of civilization included a commitment to the values of individualism, industry, and private property; the acceptance of Christian doctrine and morality, including the "Christian ideal of the family"; the abandonment of loyalty to the tribal community; . . . the willingness to become both a producer and a consumer of material goods; and finally, an acceptance of the idea that man's conquest of nature constituted one of his noblest accomplishments.

To achieve his goals, Pratt instituted a program of extreme militaristic discipline—one that served as a model for other boarding schools—that caused incalculable damage to generations of Native children. Upon their arrival to Carlisle, students had to cut their hair, which was especially disturbing to Indians given the symbolic importance of long locks. They were required to abandon their Native names and adopt Anglicized ones, as well as shed their traditional clothing and don military-style uniforms. Only English was allowed at the school; any child caught speaking his or her Native language was severely punished. Historical records show that the food was substandard and usually not provided in adequate amounts. Sanitation practices were poor as students had to share towels and drinking cups, and illnesses spread quickly as the school's leaders rarely segregated sick children. Native spirituality was completely forbidden, and the students were forced to convert to Christianity, which was part of the official curriculum. Any expression or practice of indigenous spirituality brought the most severe punishment.

As for education, the students were trained in basic English, science, and math, and also received substantial vocational training. After a half day of general education, the boys would study farming or a trade such as blacksmithing or carpentry, while the girls would learn sewing, cooking, cleaning, and nursing. It was no secret that the children were being prepared for lives as servants and laborers. Indeed, the "outing" program allowed for the students to live with nearby Anglo families during summers, assisting with household and farm duties, sometimes for a small stipend. It should come as no surprise that some of these local households viewed the Native children as free labor and often exploited and abused them.

Perhaps the most satisfying part of the boarding schools was the athletic program, with various sports made available to both boys and girls. Extracurricular activities such as school newspapers, drama, and music were available as well. Any fair examination of the boarding schools has to acknowledge these opportunities for the students, and the historical records indicate that many of the students took advantage of these activities, including the famous athlete Jim Thorpe. However, even the famed Carlisle athletic program was plagued by corruption in the later decades of the school.

But the fact that drama, sports, and choral groups were encouraged does not absolve the dehumanizing totality of these institutions and the damage done to the Native way of life. Runaway students were common at Carlisle and other boarding schools, and some institutions created jails where captured runaways were imprisoned. Other schools forced recalcitrant students into stints of hard labor or corporal punishment. There is evidence that some rebellious male students at Carlisle were hung up by their thumbs for hours. Extreme whipping and flogging, sometimes resulting in death, was common at the schools. Suicide—usually by hanging—was a frequent occurrence, and every boarding school had a cemetery on its grounds.

Heartbreakingly, the students were often tasked with building the caskets. This fact fills me with sadness as I imagine the young students sawing, sanding, and nailing the pine boxes, the final terminus for one of their friends.

There is also evidence of severe sexual abuse, and numerous lawsuits have been filed in the US and Canada alleging long-term rape and sexual molestation by teachers and administrators at various boarding and day schools. In July 2011, a Dakota man, Howard Wanna, detailed his sexual abuse at an institution in South Dakota in the magazine *Indian Country Today*. "He'd also turn me around and rape me, hurting me badly as he used his hands to grip my hair, neck, or shoulders. He rotated among about five of us younger boys, which left me with such confused emotions. On days it wasn't my turn, I was so grateful, yet I felt terrible that one of my little friends was suffering. I also dreaded the fact that my day was coming again soon."

This brief overview of boarding school life can't really do justice to the horrible and inhumane conditions there. Although there were some opportunities for students to succeed, the living conditions were generally miserable, the educational and disciplinary practices were brutal, and the entire enterprise was designed to completely eliminate the culture and spirituality of American Indians and replace it with a Western capitalistic philosophy. This is the very definition of cultural genocide.

Pratt's methods were so successful in assimilating Native children that two dozen other boarding schools were created, and Indian day schools and reservation boarding schools copied his techniques. However, Pratt was forced to retire from his position at Carlisle in 1904—his criticism of the reservation system and the Indian Bureau had proven to be too much for his superiors. He fervently believed that Natives were best served by complete assimilation into white society, to be accomplished by the dissolution of all reservations. That opinion, then and now, was not shared by many. The Carlisle

Industrial Indian School closed on September 1, 1918, becoming US Army Base Hospital Number 31.

The boarding school system continued, though, until 1928, when the Meriam Report issued a scathing critique of the schools, noting the malnutrition, poor teaching quality, and excessive disciplinary sanctions. Many of the remaining off-reservation boarding schools closed as a result, but Pratt's methods continued to be used in the reservation boarding and day schools for generations, his legacy of cultural assimilation secure.

The Carlisle Barracks remains an active military base, having served as the home of the Medical Field Service School and the US Army War College after the closing of the school, but its tragic legacy remains in what's known as the Indian Cemetery, where about two hundred children are buried. These young students died due to disease, trauma, suicide, or abuse, and school administrators—shamefully—declined to return their remains to their homelands, and often failed to notify the parents.

However, some of those children may finally be going home, as several Native nations have requested the disinterment and return of their ancestors, including the Rosebud Sioux Tribe. I spoke with Ben Rhodd, the Tribal Historic Preservation Officer for the Sicangu Lakota Nation. He said that they've identified eleven Sicangu children at the Carlisle cemetery and requested their return to South Dakota. However, he told me that their first request was denied by the Army because the tribe had not provided signed affidavits from surviving members of each child's family.

"They told us we couldn't make the request as a nation," Rhodd said. "We had to track down the living descendants and get their approval."

That's exactly what Rhodd and his team have done. They've positively identified family members for each child through painstaking research, obtained all signatures, and are now attempting to secure funding for the process, which will involve a group of people traveling to Carlisle to ensure that appropriate spiritual procedures are followed throughout the process. Rhodd told me that a medicine person will be at the Indian Cemetery and spend most nights in ceremony. Ten of the children will be draped in their own buffalo robes, but one will be enveloped in a white elk hide at the request of her family. There will then be a blessing and ceremony of thanks, and the children will be taken back to the Rosebud Reservation in a caravan.

I'm pleased to learn that these Lakota children will be returned to the reservation and their families, but it's no cause for celebration. The fact that so many Native children died—far away from home and their loved ones—fills me with sorrow, and I wonder if my grandmother lost any of her friends during her year at the school. The last student listed on the death record is Lottie Sireech, a citizen of the Ute nation, who died on January 28, 1906, four years before my grandmother Marie arrived there. But of course, the official records from the school are notoriously inaccurate.

It's important to acknowledge that my grandmother's experience at Carlisle—enrolling in the last decade of the institution—was likely somewhat different from those students who were educated at the school in its earlier decades. The institution had become less significant beginning in the early twentieth century due to the proliferation of local reservation boarding and day schools. In a sense, the popularity of Pratt's Indian educational philosophy contributed to the demise of his signature school. In the institution's final years, the student body consisted of several cohorts: orphans; children who were thought to have discipline problems; athletes; and legacies—those students whose parents had gone to the school and wanted their own children educated there. However, the educational philosophy remained largely the same. The prohibitions against speaking indigenous languages or practicing Native spirituality were still enforced, more strictly than ever. Perhaps the most noteworthy change in the post-Pratt era was a lessening of the use of corporal punishment, due to the school's second superintendent, Moses Friedman. But the policies of cultural assimilation and elimination remained largely intact.

It is difficult to reconcile the historical overview of the Indian boarding school system with the apparent positive experience of my grandmother—her longing for "Old Carlisle." Of course, it is easy to surmise that she was indoctrinated—brainwashed even—by the propaganda of the Carlisle administration and teachers. But this answer is too simple. It assumes that the Native children were modest, diffident youngsters, incapable of thinking for themselves and unwilling to assert their own opinions. This caricature doesn't fit with any Native people I've ever known. The Indians in my family are pretty stubborn and persistent, to say the least. I decided to dig deeper into some of the history of Carlisle, find out what I can about the students back then.

Barbara Landis is a historian with the Cumberland County Historical Society and one of the people who have done the most to provide access to the Carlisle School and its history. Landis is friendly and knowledgeable, and provided a great deal of information that's not present in the scholarly record. When I interviewed her by phone, we spoke about numerous topics, but my most urgent questions were regarding the issues of assimilation and acculturation—the degree to which most students at Carlisle tried to hold on to their traditions.

In response, Landis told me of the interview she conducted with the last living female Carlisle student, ninety-nine-year-old Maggie Tarbell, who spoke of her days at the school before it closed. Tarbell recounted that she would sneak into her room and "talk Indian" with other students as an act of resistance and rebellion. But Landis noted, "She always ended any story she told us with these words: 'It was a good school and I got a good education there.' We were asking pretty leading questions, but I think she felt like these two white women were coming to check on her, and so the company line came back to her." The company line. Even eighty years after leaving Carlisle, Tarbell felt the need to protect the school and echo the words they'd been taught.

Then I shared with Landis the alumna note my grandmother had sent to the student newspaper, the one where she longs for "Old Carlisle," and I expressed my dismay that my grandmother apparently liked the institution rather than acting as an agent of resistance, the role I'd have preferred she play.

"She was probably following the line she learned. The language of complacency and endearment. That's not genuine," Landis said.

"What do you mean by 'line'?" I asked.

"The company line. It's like the, uhh, when someone gets kidnapped."

"Stockholm syndrome," I said.

"Yes, exactly."

There was silence for a moment as I processed what Landis had told me. In that instant, the disappointment I'd been carrying largely vanished, as I realized that my grandmother was also echoing the Carlisle line in her correspondence. Toeing the company line was a concept with which I was quite familiar, as well as the rationalizations that accompany those actions. It was unfair of me to hold her to a higher standard, especially given the level of indoctrination she'd experienced while at Carlisle.

Near the end of our conversation, Landis recommended that I look at the student publications that are now digitized and available online in order to get a sense of the propaganda to which the students were exposed. I quickly located the digital archive and was surprised by the sheer number of documents available. Student records, photographs, historical documents, school publications. The official publication list alone has twelve different titles from different eras of the school. The *Carlisle Arrow*, the *Indian Craftsman*, the *Indian Helper*, the *Morning Star*, and the *Red Man* are just a few of the newspapers and journals the students worked to publish and distribute.

I was delighted to connect with the words of these Native young people of the past and eager to read their thoughts and opinions. I started with the *Red Man*. This student-edited journal published articles from various sources outside of the school as well as student-written commentary. Randomly, I found an article that is indicative of the attitudes of the time, an essay from June 1912 entitled "Sanitary Homes for Indians" by one Edgar B. Meritt. He was not a Carlisle student or a Native, but worked as a law clerk for the Indian Bureau.

In his article, he argued that Indians should abandon their traditional housing structures for standard Western homes (and even included blueprints for said houses):

> There are to-day thousands of Indians who are wards of the Government living from four to eight to the family in one-room shacks, cabins, wickiups, or tents, some of them on dirt floors, and under the most revolting, unsanitary conditions— conditions that must of necessity cause the propagation and transmission of most dangerous diseases, such as tuberculosis and trachoma, not only to each member of the Indian family, but to other Indians of the immediate vicinity, as well as the whites with whom they come in contact.

This horseshit isn't surprising, but is still appalling, given that traditional Native homes were exactly the opposite of what the author contends—clean, safe, and environmentally friendly—and served Indians well for tens of thousands of years before the arrival of the settlers and their diseases. I wondered how the student journalists felt about this piece, whether they were again spouting the company line or if they truly believed that their traditional homes were breeding grounds for disease.

I turned then to the student newspaper the *Carlisle Arrow*, which focused on alumni and student news rather than longer essays and features. I opened up the issue from September 1910, likely the first one that my grandmother read upon her arrival to Carlisle. It was written in a cheery, snappy style, and the school news section resembled the alumni news columns from the college newsletters I receive. As I scanned more issues, the phrase "Old Carlisle" came up again and again in alumni notes, and I saw how deeply rooted the process of indoctrination was for the students. "Louis Dupuis, Class '11, from his home in Horton, Kans., writes: 'I often think of dear old Carlisle and wish I were there.' " Charles Dagenett, Class '89, reported, "I am ever thankful to old Carlisle for having taught me my trade. I am endeavoring to make use of it and by constant practice am adding a little to it all the time. I am enjoying splendid health here and am not confined to the office all the time. I keep a team and buggy which affords us much healthful pleasure. I am ever mindful of the Captain's kindness to me."

But from my previous research, I knew that there had been significant acts of rebellion and resistance by some Carlisle students who were less enamored of Captain Pratt's kindness. The scholarly books I'd read had documented numerous acts of student agency and resistance, including running away, violent and passive resistance to school rules, and secret gatherings where the students would conduct Native religious ceremonies. David Wallace Adams in *Education for Extinction* discusses an incident at Carlisle in 1897 where two female students, one Lakota and one Menominee, lit the school on fire—twice—before being caught and confessing to the arson. Rather than deal with the girls himself, Pratt turned them over to local prosecutors and they were convicted and sentenced to eighteen months in the penitentiary. I appreciate the girls' spirit, if not their method, but it's hard to imagine how they fared in the state prison for a year and a half.

I'd like to think that my grandmother tried to hold on to her culture and resist some of the Carlisle policies, but of course, there's no way to know if that ever happened. Barbara Landis had told me one other thing, a fact that I'd not read anywhere else. She'd said that by the twentieth century, the Carlisle Indian School was considered to be the elite institution of all of the boarding schools, and that some students derived status from their time there when they returned home. In fact, Landis said that they were called "Carlisle girls" by some, and an elder had told her, "You could always pick out the Carlisle girls. They had a way about them."

As much as I'd like to think that my grandmother had resisted the school administration to some degree, it's entirely possible she'd viewed her attendance at Carlisle as a prize, something of which to be proud, one of her great accomplishments. She spent just one year at the Carlisle School, not returning, presumably, because of her marriage to my grandfather.

Shortly after our interview, Landis sent me a list of documents from Carlisle—newspaper items, official documents—in which my grandmother appeared. I learn that, on her trip to Pennsylvania, she was accompanied by five girls and six boys, and that the family of one of those girls, Amy Gunhammer, would later send a letter to Carlisle accusing the school of keeping their daughter as a prisoner and demanding her release. I also learn from the documents that Marie later wrote to the *Carlisle Arrow* telling of the dressmaking skills she'd learned there. I see four more alumna notes where she'd written to update her classmates. In the February 18, 1916 edition of the *Carlisle Arrow*, this item appeared: "Mrs. Clarence Cordry, née Marie Beauvais, writes that she is now located at Wood, S. Dak. She is keeping house for her husband, who is employed as farmer on the Rosebud Reservation."

I also find an item from her school days and see that she had been a bridesmaid during her last months at Carlisle for a friend, Margaretta Reed, for her marriage to another Carlisle student, Lewis George. This suggests that she made friends easily during her one year at Carlisle. The note fills me with delight as I try to imagine the little ceremony at the school, the vows and best wishes, the future looming ahead of everyone. The newspaper reported that, "The ceremony was witnessed by a large audience of schoolmates and friends. The bride was attired in blue silk and wore a wreath of orange blossoms. The two bridesmaids, Miss Marie Beauvais and Miss Nora McFarland, were attired in white and wore white veils . . . . After the ceremony a reception was given by Superintendent and Mrs. Friedman for the bridal party and their friends, after which amid a shower of rice and good wishes, the bride and groom departed for their future home in California."

I like to think that she was happy during her time at Carlisle, that it was a time of friends and fellowship, and that she was excited by her prospects—those vistas of possibility—in front of her. Of course, I know of the sadnesses she endured in later years: thirteen children to raise; a dead husband; her favorite daughter and grandchild murdered; and her final years in that tiny shack on the reservation. I hope those months at Carlisle were enough to sustain her over the long haul of family life, grinding poverty, and the chasms of grief we all must face when a loved one dies.

I stand with my cousin James in South Dakota and we discuss our grandmother. He's one of the last descendants of Marie Beauvais still living on the reservation, and, being a decade older than me, he remembers more, knows more. We're at the ruins of her little cabin, where her decades of "keeping house" came to a bitter end.

"It doesn't make sense," I say, looking at the wreckage of her shack. "How could her children leave her here? Why didn't any of them take her in, let her stay with them? I know some of them had decent houses."

"No," he says, shaking his head. "You don't get it. She *wanted* to be here. She insisted on living here. This is where she wanted to be."

As the enormity of this sinks in, I slowly begin to understand. My grandmother resisted the entreaties of her children to live with them, and she chose to return to the land, living as her ancestors had done. This was her reclamation of Native identity, her last act of resistance, a final rebellion as she sought peace at the end of her life.

I think of her there, surrounded by the land, the silence enveloping her, and I hope that she heard the voices, the voices of her parents, siblings, children, grandchildren, and also the happy murmurs of her classmates at Carlisle, as she sat there alone, finally alone.

Later that day, I go to the little cemetery on the reservation where she and the rest of my family are buried. Grandmother, grandfather, aunts, uncles, and my cousin Gregory, murdered at age twelve, the same age as my youngest son. Emotion overcomes me as I realize all that's been lost, and I'm weeping for Marie, for Gregory, and for those students buried at Carlisle who will never come home. My grandmother longed for Old Carlisle, yes, but I believe that she longed for the time before the sorrows came, the time when she wandered the grassy hills of the Rosebud, her sisters and brothers at her side, the prairie stretching out before her.

The sun begins to set as I stand there, the shadows lengthening and the clouds gathering. I'm alone on this trip, but I'll bring my sons next time and force them to put down their gadgets for a few days. We'll visit these graves and burn some sage, then I'll take them to the ruins of Marie's little shack and tell them all I know about her. How she lived and how she died. The stories of Carlisle and the stories of the Lakota people. We'll shake off the city and look out into the horizon to the very edge of the reservation.

STEVEN COLE HUGHES

A Brief History of Banned Books
a 10-minute play

CHARACTERS

ISHMAEL	20s–50s, any gender, any ethnicity
LYRA	20s–50s, any gender, any ethnicity
SKIP	20s–50s, any gender, any ethnicity

SETTING

A bookstore. The near future.

BOOKS DISCUSSED IN THIS PLAY

His Dark Materials – Moby Dick – The Adventures of Huckleberry Finn – The Autobiography of Malcom X – Beloved – The Catcher in the Rye – Fahrenheit 451 – Harry Potter – Where the Sidewalk Ends – The Art of the Deal – The Art of War – Unlikeable: The Problem with Hillary

A BOOKSTORE. THE NEAR FUTURE.

ISHMAEL *stands in front of a bookshelf, talking to LYRA and SKIP.*

ISHMAEL

Hi. Welcome. Thank you for coming. I know it probably wasn't easy getting here. My name is Ishmael. So . . . you can . . . call me Ishmael. That's a little literary joke. So . . .

OK, let's just dive right in: this is a bookstore. Well, this is a replica of a bookstore. We . . .

OK, so, let's go back to the end of the last century. Amazon was founded in 1994 as a website that sold books. Thirty years later they had put all other booksellers in the United States out of business. People were still reading books, they just weren't going to actual bookstores anymore. The real threat to books themselves came when—I'm sorry, there are so few of you here, I feel like I should have you introduce yourselves.

(To LYRA.)

Hi.

LYRA
Hi. My name is Lyra.

ISHMAEL
Lyra. Like Lyra Belacqua.

LYRA
Yes, exactly.

ISHMAEL
Really?

LYRA
Yes, my parents read books. We had a secret stash in the basement growing up.

ISHMAEL
That's great.

LYRA
Have you ever read *His Dark Materials*?

ISHMAEL

Yes, of course, I love it! So, you were named for Lyra from *His Dark Materials*?

LYRA

Yes.

ISHMAEL

Cool.

LYRA

And, presumably your parents read *Moby Dick*?

ISHMAEL

Yes, they did.

LYRA

Cool.

ISHMAEL

So, we're both named for literary heroes.

LYRA

Yes.

ISHMAEL

Cool!

(*To SKIP.*)

And you?

SKIP

My name is Skip.

ISHMAEL

OK. Hi, Skip. Welcome.

SKIP

Thank you.

ISHMAEL

OK, so, where was I? Um . . . so, I want to talk about banned books. Let's start by talking about Our Leader. -

SKIP

He's a very stable genius.

LYRA

He's a very stable genius.

ISHMAEL

He's a very stable genius.

(Pause. They all look at each other.)

So . . . I assume that you both found your way here by . . . certain . . . underground . . . means . . . so . . . what we talk about next might get a little . . . well, I'll just . . .

This country has a long history of banning books. The two most frequently banned books of all time are *The Adventures of Huckleberry Finn* by Mark Twain, banned because it was too anti-Black; and *The Autobiography of Malcolm X* by Malcolm X, banned because it was too anti-white. So.

Then, of course, we have *Beloved* by Toni Morrison, banned because it was too sexy; *Catcher in the Rye* by J.D. Salinger, banned because it was too obscene; and *Fahrenheit 451* by Ray Bradbury, banned because it was a book about banning books.

In the early 2000s, the *Harry Potter* series of fantasy books by J.K. Rowling were challenged by religious groups for promoting Occultism and Satanism.

LYRA
Wow.

ISHMAEL
I know, right? Have you ever read a *Harry Potter* book?

LYRA
All seven of them.

ISHMAEL
Really?

LYRA
Yeah.

ISHMAEL
Wow. I've only ever been able to get my hands on the first one.

LYRA
Oh, you've got to read them all. They're wonderful.

ISHMAEL
How about you, Skip?

(*They both look at SKIP.*)

SKIP
How about me, what?

ISHMAEL

Have you ever read any of the *Harry Potter* books?

SKIP

Oh. Uh . . . no.

ISHMAEL

OK . . . You're starting to make me nervous, Skip. You're not an Administration spy, are you? Ha ha!

LYRA

Ha ha!

SKIP

Ha ha!

(ISHMAEL and LYRA are both looking at SKIP.)

No, I'm not.

ISHMAEL

OK . . . so, what brought you here today, Skip? Do you have a favorite book?

SKIP

Oh, um, I like all of the . . . fiction . . . books.

ISHMAEL

All of the fiction books?

SKIP

Yes . . .

LYRA

What was your favorite book as a child?

SKIP

Oh, I don't . . .

ISHMAEL

Did your parents read to you?

SKIP

Yes. They did. My mother read me . . . *Where the Sidewalk Ends.*

ISHMAEL & LYRA

Ohhhh.

ISHMAEL

That's great.

LYRA

Wonderful.

ISHMAEL

Cool. Thanks. Great. OK, let's get back to . . . so, after Our Leader was—

SKIP

He's a very stable genius.

LYRA

He's a very stable genius.

ISHMAEL

He's a very stable genius.

(*Pause. They all look at each other.*)

LYRA

You know, I'm actually OK if we don't incant. If you guys are OK
with it. I mean, it's just the three of us, so . . .

ISHMAEL

I'm OK not doing it. I was just doing it because I thought . . .

LYRA

Yeah, no, of course . . .

SKIP

Maybe we should incant. Just in case.

LYRA

OK . . .

ISHMAEL

Actually, it will kind of get in the way of the presentation if we
have to incant each time I say his name, so, is it OK with you, Skip,
if we don't?

(LYRA looks at SKIP.)

SKIP

OK.

ISHMAEL

OK. So . . .

In 2020, the Administration started to officially ban books that
contained any unflattering references to Our Leader.

As the civil unrest of the Twenties reached a climax, the Administration banned all books that it deemed controversial: books that

contained liberal political thought; books that promoted homo-sexuality and/or gender, racial, or religious equality; and anything written by Ta-Nehisi Coates.

When Our Leader declared himself Benevolent Protector and Uniter of the United States of America Except California in 2024, the Administration shut down all newspapers, universities, libraries, and the remaining brick and mortar Amazon bookstores. Fox News took control of the Amazon website and turned it into State Run Media, where the only three books citizens were allowed to buy and read were *The Art of the Deal* by Our Leader, *The Art of War* by Sun Tzu, and *Unlikeable: The Problem with Hillary* by Ed Klein.

The Free State of California still had universities and libraries and independent bookstores until the War of 2025. After the war, some brave librarians and professors smuggled books out of the ashes of California to a vast underground network in the rest of the country.

Bookstore museums started, obviously, in Portland, then spread to Chicago and New York City. Museums are now popping up in Boston, Ann Arbor, Denver . . .

We call ourselves The Free Librarians.

SKIP

That's it, I've heard enough! Ishmael, you're under arrest according to the Prior Restraint and Unity Act of 2030.

ISHMAEL

I knew it!

LYRA

Skip—

SKIP

(Pulls out a ridiculous-looking futuristic laser gun.)

Don't move! Either of you.

ISHMAEL

She's not a part of this. Let her go!

SKIP

Stop talking!

LYRA

Skip, please, don't do this . . .

SKIP

You both talk too much! Now, look, you seem like a nice person, Lyra. I don't want to hurt you. So, just, Ishmael, you come with me.

ISHMAEL

You don't have to do this.

SKIP

Don't make me set my laser gun to Big League!

LYRA

Skip—

SKIP

Lyra, stay out of this! Ishmael, you're a bad hombre!

LYRA

He's not a bad hombre just because he reads.

SKIP

Our country is post-literate.

ISHMAEL

We don't have to be.

SKIP

We must unify!

LYRA

By not reading?

SKIP

By not reading lies.

LYRA

Picasso said art is the lie that tells the truth.

SKIP

That doesn't make any sense!

ISHMAEL

It's a metaphor.

SKIP

That word is forbidden!

ISHMAEL

I know.

SKIP

Lies can't tell the truth! That's liberal indoctrination. There are lies told by journalists and professors and authors, and there's the truth told by Our Leader. He's a very stable genius.

LYRA

Skip, listen to yourself.

SKIP

Listen to *yourself*!

LYRA

OK.

SKIP

OK.

LYRA

What am I listening to?

SKIP

What? Nothing. Stop talking! Ishmael, you're coming with me. Lyra, you need to leave. I'm calling in an airstrike on this bookstore museum.

LYRA

No, you can't do that!

ISHMAEL

Lyra, just go.

LYRA

No.

SKIP

If you don't leave, I'll have to arrest you too, and no one hates imprisoning women more than Our Leader. He's a very stable genius.

ISHMAEL

Go, Lyra. Get out of here.

LYRA

No!

SKIP

Go!

LYRA

Hear your mother's voice.

SKIP

What?

LYRA

Hear the sound of your mother's voice reading *Where the Sidewalk Ends* to you.

SKIP

No . . .

LYRA

How does it begin?

SKIP

I don't remember.

LYRA

Yes, you do. How does it begin?

SKIP

Stop . . .

LYRA

If you are a dreamer, come in.

SKIP

Stop it.

LYRA

If you are a dreamer, a wisher, a liar.

SKIP

Stop . . .

LYRA

Say it with me . . .

LYRA & SKIP

If you're a hope-er, a pray-er, a magic bean buyer . . .

> *(SKIP lowers his laser gun. He stumbles into LYRA'S arms. They collapse onto the floor together. She cradles him.)*

SKIP

Read to me, Mama.

LYRA

> *(Whispering, to ISHMAEL.)*

Go.

ISHMAEL

No.

SKIP

Mama?

LYRA

If you're a pretender, come sit by my fire.

(To ISHMAEL.)

Go, now. You're too important. Bookstores are too important.

ISHMAEL

I . . .

LYRA

Go!

ISHMAEL

I'll never forget you, Lyra.

LYRA

I'll never forget you, Ishmael.

ISHMAEL

And I only am escaped alone to tell thee. Herman Melville. *Moby Dick.*

LYRA

So Lyra and her daemon turned away from the world they were born in, and looked toward the sun, and walked into the sky. Philip Pullman. *His Dark Materials.*

(ISHMAEL runs out.)

SKIP

Mama?

LYRA

I'm here, Skip.

SKIP

Read me another story.

> *(LYRA pulls a book, any book, off the shelf and opens it. SKIP looks up at LYRA and almost comes out of his trance for a moment.)*

SKIP

He's a very stable—

LYRA

Shh . . .

SKIP

He's a very—

LYRA

Shhhh . . .

SKIP

He's a—

LYRA

Shhhhhh . . .

SKIP

He's—

LYRA

Shhhhhhhh . . .

End of Play

ADDIE TSAI

Writing as a Vessel for Chaos:
A Letter to High Schoolers

I remember the moment I realized, seriously, that I wanted to be a writer. It wasn't the first time I wrote something for an audience, although that did something to me, too. That was a different kind of moment, one that was tinged with external validation, something I lacked in my young life (I was in third grade, and I'd received an award for a Mother's Day poem I wrote in order to make my mother—who was elusive and sparkly, suddenly appearing and vanishing just that quickly like a rainbow on a day of showers in the spring—happy enough so that she would stay). But the moment I realized I wanted to pursue writing as a lifelong practice—perhaps, I thought, like someone pursues a religious faith—happened when I was a sophomore in high school, and it happened because of an English assignment.

To say this now seems like such a cliché, but it's true. I am the writer I am today because of the teachers who made me believe that to follow this frustrating, aching, necessary, glorious, painful, dissatisfying, and endlessly life-affirming work was something I had a kind of propensity for. And that is because I explicitly did not have the kind of parents or guardians or other figures in my life from whom I could have believed in myself to do just about anything. It's probably worth noting here that I didn't think much of this teacher. To be honest, I didn't even like her. But she gave me an assignment that changed my life—and not only because it encouraged me to follow writing, but also because the assignment itself provided me with a lifesaving coping mechanism. At the time, I could feel something incredibly healing happening to me, although I wouldn't understand exactly what, or how, until much later: until after I began therapy, until I started to carve out a consciousness for how trauma impacts the brain and the body, how processing one's feelings and experiences regarding pain can be a kind of regenerative practice for surviving and remaking the self that has had to navigate immense damage as one develops into an adult.

We'd just finished reading *Oedipus Rex*, and I remember being quite taken with it. The teacher asked us to write a poem about the symbolism of Oedipus, but her one stipulation was that it couldn't rhyme. I had no idea poems existed that didn't rhyme. I recall scoffing about it to my mother on the phone (I'm not sure what city she was in, or whether she was at her apartment where I lived but did not often live with her at the time).

At the same time, I was trying to navigate experiences laced with childhood abuse that were becoming increasingly untenable—some of these experiences directly happened to me, but those that were almost more difficult were the ones impacting my twin sister and my older brother, and that I was forced to witness while remaining silent, and feeling that silence was a matter of my survival. It was an impossible double-bind to watch my brother and sister be abused and feel there was nothing I could do to stop it. Even though I, too, was the victim of abuse, much of my teenage years were framed and defined by what I couldn't prevent from happening to my siblings. I had fantasies as the abuse was happening where I would scream at my dominant, protective, reliable, hyper-alarmist, loving, narcissistic, terrifying father to stop what he was doing, to point to my brother's face, splotchy face red from crying and fear. But just like he held my brother's face while threatening him for doing poorly in school, or for the number of other illogical *reasons* that he would claim provoked his rage, that time, this time, the other time, the many, many times, my father also would hold the mouths of my words in my own throat, snuffed into silence, relegated to a fantasy that I never felt courageous enough to act on. Even as witnessing my brother in terror and pain destroyed me inside.

I decided I would use this Oedipus assignment to write about what I had experienced, what I struggled to witness. It was a revelation to me—therapy before I would find (and be able to afford) therapy—and set me on a journey toward healing the wounds that could have otherwise stopped me dead in my tracks in more ways than one. I'm not even sure I could explain what it did to channel all that I couldn't say in a poem. I'm sure I was terrified, at least a little, to share it with my fellow students and my teacher, but the writing of it had been, suddenly, such a profound and powerful experience that my desire to share it with others, to have them witness and acknowledge my pain and my expression, became greater than my fear at having my deepest secrets exposed.

A House in Silence

As the sun's rays flood through the windows,
A sky of autumn sets the world to sleep with tones of scarlets and violets.
Just as the doors are locked and the lights dimmed low,
A house rests, silently chaotic.
Inside, children, like two tiny mice, welcome the darkness
And shudder with the fear of the inevitable.
A single slap
Dissolves the safety of the house
with the denial of a single hand.
The face turns scarlet with heat and the eyes fill with a black lividness.
The boy bears a shadow of navy and coal.

This horror is a virus slowly casting a shadow over the house
From the red-brick chimney to the gardens,
Filled with flowers and trees.
Roses and apples tilt in the wind,
Swaying in full view, and gently swish the window,
Blind to the lives inside.

Like a heavy quilt, Fatigue slowly covers the living room,
Breathing an exhausted sigh
For the withering of fear and the tense serenity.
The children creep out,
And, as swiftly as a tide, it is over,
The wave of anger has washed over the house,
Leaving its mark.

The teacher took me aside on the day she passed them back and suggested that I submit it to the contest for the literary journal on campus. I didn't win, or even get asked to publish it. But I'd remember that I had confided to her, in my own way, my darkest secrets, and she had not rejected me. Not only that, but she had validated me, and validated the art that I was making out of my life. There would be other mentors, other teachers down the line who would do something similar for me, but she was the first one to show me that I could use the poem as the vessel for trying to understand the chaos that was my life then. It is a practice I have never forgotten, and it will always be the most important aspect of what writing is to me—more important than fame or publication.

CAROLINA EBEID

Punctum / Metaphora

Love remains a kind of present tense. This is how we describe the scenes in photographs—as though the actions in them were still happening. My father is throwing a rock in this picture. My father keeps lions in his chest & they rip apart a gazelle in this picture.

A man throwing a rock; the image holds an old grammar. This rock has yet to leave the hand, to measure the horizontal span from A to B. Nor has it completed the vertical distance from first line to last line, riding a tangle of syntax. The photograph captures a skirmish in the West Bank town of Nablus; the man hurling the rock is my father insofar as Juliet is the sun.

Punctum / Image of an Intifada

And then you were standing under a red arcade of flyers. The military
said it dispersed leaflets over Gaza warning residents to keep away—
leaflets, I wanted to say, fell like autumn, an artificial autumn in a
school play, & we know it's a tragicomedy because the dead lovers
get up again—

Abid for the adorer, worshipper, he gets up again, the anonymous
one, *Munhit* whose voice is in his chest, the man throwing a rock,
my husband, *Samer* who talks smoothly at night, I am a perfect wife
to a revolution, he is a chain-link fence collecting snow, *Sildin* who
doesn't care what happens, he is a black-figure athlete on a water jug
in a museum, *Hamza* who won't let go, *father*, I call out to him, *Khalil*
is the beautiful friend, he is a squeaky pink balloon twisted & twisted
into an elephant—what will you name him?

Palestine, the Metaphor

Palestine, the metaphor, says to me

not, I'll not, Palestine the future country,
not Palestine the vehicle,

holy o most holy, I'll not theater
the Palestine, not otherwise it, nor

tempest it green & black & red
& black & ash & black war,

I'll not war, Palestine is not a war,
no six day victor come,

no seventh day, its waste of daffodils.

Punctum / The Transom

There is a quality about the rectangular shape of a stanza that is suggestive of a window pane, a sheet of glass through which we can see into another place. I sit up in bed reading when I should be sleeping. It's a comfort to think that somewhere another person is also sitting up in bed reading, not sleeping. And surely, tonight, in yet another bed a woman wants her eyes to be windows into the soul, but no one looks in. For the span of five minutes I thought, I had all those years misunderstood the concept of the eyes being windows. And I was delighted: yes, I said, the eyes are windows *for* the soul, the soul is what stares out of them, safely inside the room of you. And then it was gone, the excitement, the long syllable of thought. And in its wake what had that been, a poem? just a room for being, in that night there of no sleep?

Now I am in an altogether other room, this one filled with daylight. There's a tall window, & above it a second window facing heavenward, & what if you won't give me heaven?—then let's call it the realm of heat & weather systems churning. Can I say it out loud? The poem is that window, and you, the reader, the beautiful friend looking out.

Punctum / Sawing a Woman in Half

I ride a glorious bus. It is a metaphorical bus, or perhaps, after all, it's a machine for metaphor-making. Yes, a gospel tallyho. It stays put. It doesn't take to the highway, but it carries me places. I rev it up & it purrs out a line about Juliet. She's a bright golden ball of nuclear fire. A way of apprehending the world. My sun. My only son, now seven, teaches me a new measure: drop everything, sit on the floor & play. See it turn & turn, the red veronicas, sometimes something sharp & wounding behind his cape. When I see a blouse on a clothesline, or man's shirt next to a blouse drying outside on a stretch of cord in between the buildings, & there is wind enough so that they swing up together, & the cuff of the man's shirt grazes the cuff of the blouse, that's when I believe in the soul. My beautiful friend, Khalil, warns me it's a problem to appropriate a spirit animal, though you have to identify, he says, where your spirit belongs: water, air, or land? I think instead I have a spirit fruit. My spirit pricks like a pineapple. How it keeps growing fat in the dark. Gold & rank. A song playing in the next apartment can dismantle me. I care less & less about being beautiful. I care everyday about being less & less beautiful. When I look at an MRI of my brain, I do not believe in the soul. I love mornings because of the coffee & the possibilities. I continue to believe that poetry contains revolutionary power. Small talk is an art & best performed in the small hours with another naked in bed. I believe the most beautiful thought is that of a holy transfiguration.

STEVEN DUNN

Intro / An Excerpt from *Travel with Nas*

I grew up in a small town in West Virginia: Kimball (population 500). I read a lot before going to middle school, but outside of textbooks and newspapers, I read only one book from the ages of 12–21. I'm a novelist now, a Creative Writing professor, and I write book reviews.

Reading only one book was partly an institutional fault, and partly my fault:

Partly my fault because I cared more about math, painting, and maps.

Partly an institutional fault because of poverty. And we were assigned only one lil funky-ass book throughout middle and high school: *The Old Man and the Sea*. We watched *Of Mice and Men*, *Grapes of Wrath*, and *Little Women*. I hated English classes because they were mostly about correcting our language by prescribing us with ways to speak. We learned that the generations of language we celebrated in, cried in, analyzed with, and joked in was wrong. And the books were about white people and white problems and white triumphs and white hopes and white dreams. So I was like, "Fuck English and literature and all that white bullshit." I was right. And I was wrong.

I was wrong about English and literature because of course Black people had been writing literature about us, I just didn't know shit about it, and them white folks ain't care enough to teach it. I was right because I was listening to rap. And I was wrong because I was listening to rap.

What I mean is, I was right about disregarding white English and white literature because rap was about Black problems, Black triumphs, Black hopes, and Black dreams. I was wrong to disregard literature in general because rap is literature, but none of my English teachers then would've called it that, or treated it as such. But I learned just as much, if not more, about social studies, geography, and language from rap albums than I did from school. And rap albums were not about correcting Black speech—they valued all its inventiveness, flexibility, warmth, and urgency. Rap albums were spaces for me to learn without feeling like shit because of the way I talked. Plus, I got to see that the way I talked was smart as hell, contemplative, and caring.

The summer after third grade was when I first heard "I Got it Made," and my man Special Ed said, "I'm outspoken, my language is broken into a slang, but it's just a dialect that I select when I hang." I had never heard the word dialect in my life, so I looked it up (because my grandma made me, like she did every time we asked her what a word meant): *a particular form of a language which is peculiar to a specific region or social group.* In the first verse Special Ed said he had the gift of speech. So boom, that was it for me: Slang was a gift of speech that we use when we hang with our friends.

That following school year, we had to write one of them lil pages about what we did over the summer. I wrote that I was cold maxin' with my crew in New York and I ain't have nothing but fun to da max. That was true: We took a Greyhound to Yonkers to visit my aunts and cousins.

My teacher went off on me in front of the class. She said that "ain't" and "da" weren't words, that there was no such thing as "cold maxin,'" and that I needed to learn proper English. I looked her dead in her punk-ass face and said, "Look, my language is broken into a slang. It's just a dialect that I select when I hang."

That same year (1989), I was obsessed with the "Just a Friend" video by Biz Markie. We were also learning all the state capitals. North Dakota's capital was Bismarck. So in my eight-year-old mind, the connection was obvious. I looked up Bismarck in the encyclopedia (again because my grandma made me) but I ain't pay attention to shit but the trees and the brick capitol building. I wrote a letter, straight up addressed on the envelope: To: North Dakota Fr: Steven Dunn

Dear North Dakota,

Thank you for naming your state capital after my favorite rapper Biz Markie. I am glad y'all let him have his video at the capitol building and he was sitting on the bench with his friends. It was easy for me to remember your capital. Please tell Biz Markie I said hello and I'm sorry his girlfriend kissed another boy.

Outtie 5000,

Steven "MC Lil Steve" Dunn

I walked down the hill to the post office and slid that envelope—with no postage or return address—into that big-ass blue mailbox. Then I got my grandma's mail, and a money order, went to the other store to play her numbers, then walked back home beaming like, Yeeeahh nigga, maybe mama can take me to North Dakota so I can make a song with Biz Markie.

All of that is to say that I was already tuned to language and places through rap by the time I hit seventh grade when Nas dropped *Illmatic*. Then the summer before tenth grade when he dropped *It Was Written*. Then twelfth grade in 1999 when he dropped *I Am* . . . Then right after I got out of boot camp the same year, he dropped *Nastradamus*. *Stillmatic* in 2001. *God's Son* in 2002. All of them albums came out during my ages of 12–21. I have to take back my statement about reading only one book from ages 12–21, because Nas's albums are books. Which means that I read at least six more books goddammit.

Because I was always rapping and shit at home, my grandma would be like, "If you knew your schoolwork like you knew them damn rap songs, you'd be a genius." If she was still alive she'd be pretty happy that now, these rap songs *are* my schoolwork.

Nas's songs made me imagine places I'd never been, and never thought of, but dreamed of visiting. His songs made me research places. They made me look up people I'd never knew but sounded important. I didn't know of Michael Eric Dyson until Nas shouted him out in 2004 on *Street's Disciple's* "These are our Heroes." So I started reading Dyson. And six years later in 2010, Dyson and Sohail Daulatzai published this cool-ass collection of scholarly essays presenting *Illmatic* from an academic perspective, called *Born to Use Mics: Reading Nas's Illmatic.* Y'all should read that shit if you haven't. *Born To Use Mics* is my book's uncle and auntie. And I hope there are more book cousins and homies about Nas because I wished somebody woulda taught some Nas books and albums while I was in school.

For the last 26 years Nas's storytelling always had me leaning my ear to the speaker like, Oooh I can't wait to see what this story is! He creates atmospheric narratives and scenes and fills them with layers of details and dialogue.

In his verse, Nas says that Shorty Doo-Wop is twelve years old. I was thirteen at the time, which made me feel like Shorty. I mean, I wasn't shooting at anybody or selling crack, but I was doing other dumb shit, and that moment captured when my older cousins or uncles sat me down to tell me some shit I needed to hear. That scene made me feel included. And I knew I ain't wanna end up like Shorty Doo-Wop.

Then in 1998 when I saw the movie *Belly* (starring Nas and DMX), that same scene was filmed—Nas and lil twelve-year-old Shorty Doo-Wop sitting on a bench in the projects having the same convo from the song. Me and my cousin looked at each other and was like, "Nigga that's the scene from "One Love"!" We paused the VHS, pulled out the *Illmatic* CD, *boop boop boop* to track 7, then listened to "One Love" again to see how close the film was to the song. Perfect! Except in the film Nas had on a white jacket instead of a black army suit like he said in the song, but we ain't care. That shit has been stuck with me forever like, this nigga Nas wrote a rap song so detailed that somebody was able to film it. I've always wanted more of that, to be able to experience Nas's stories materialized into another format. So Imma do that shit in here too. I'll be adapting some of Nas's storytelling songs into stories on the page so y'all can also experience them. I said above that Nas's albums are books, so outside of straight pleasure, me adapting the songs will also highlight their literary elements.

Alright, since y'all here with me, we finna do this schoolwork. In addition to me adapting songs, we finna look at the structures and mechanisms of some of his lyrics. We finna listen to Nas's own insights about his process and places. We finna use Nas's specific geographies to create doorways of inquiry into history and other areas of sociality. Meaning we gonna travel to a lot of the places throughout his discography. Nas writes *from* those places instead of *about* those places. Like in "Sekou Story" from *Street's Disciple*, he doesn't just mention Miami, he gets in the guts of the city by naming Nikki Beach, Coconut Grove, and Biscayne Bay. And he's not just naming those places, he offers narratives reinforced by montage-like movements, like in "N.Y. State of Mind Part 2": "Broken glass in the hallway, bloodstained floors, neighbors look at every bag you bring through your doors, lock the top lock, mama should've cuffed me to the radiator." Everything feels real, which in turn makes us feel like we are also there.

PART II

Body

KRISTEN IVERSEN

When Death Came to Golden

In June 1977, following my first year of college, I took a job driving a roach coach, an old converted pickup truck that brought food to workers at construction sites near my neighborhood just outside Denver. The truck was white with diamond-patterned aluminum doors on both sides that swung up to expose ice chests filled with sodas and half-pint cardboard cartons of milk. I sold stale ham sandwiches, Cokes, and MoonPies to boys just a few years older than I was, boys who were shirtless and muscled and hungry. One day a new boy, a shy boy, bought a sandwich and, as soon as the other boys had walked away, asked if I might want to meet for dinner. Mark was quiet and polite and seemed a little lost. I said yes. We met at an Italian restaurant, where we sat on the patio under a moonlit sky. Over pepperoni pizza, our first-date conversation turned intimate and intense. Abruptly he leaned forward, his brown eyes troubled, and told me his sister had disappeared two years earlier. For months no one knew where she was. And then she was found dead.

Mark said Shelley was tall like me, five eight or so, with hazel eyes and long brown hair parted in the middle. She was slim and pretty in a girl-next-door kind of way. The day she disappeared, she was wearing what we all wore back then: bell-bottom jeans, a T-shirt with the name of a rock band on the front—maybe *Yes* or *Emerson, Lake & Palmer*—and hiking boots. Hiking boots were de rigueur for Colorado girls. We were tough. We were untethered. We reveled in all the freedoms the sixties and seventies seemed to promise young girls like us. We tried smoking pot and backpacking and sleeping with boys, things our mothers never did. We thought about medical school or law school, even though our families couldn't afford it, even though our fathers disapproved. Hitchhiking was common. Everyone did it. You could hitch from Denver to Boulder or Boulder to Birmingham or ride all the way to the West Coast if you wanted.

Like Shelley, I wore my hair parted in the middle, long and straight down my back.

It turns out Ted Bundy preferred women with long hair parted in the middle.

Police found a gas receipt from a station in Golden, dated just days before Shelley disappeared, crumpled under the passenger seat of Bundy's white VW Bug. Twenty minutes from Denver, Golden is the self-proclaimed Gateway to the Rockies. Winding neighborhoods rise into the foothills backed by the first row of the Rocky Mountains, dark blue and green, a jagged spine extending along the horizon. The town is filled with taverns, coffee shops, pizza parlors, and back then, the historic Foss drugstore, now gone. Golden has been a company town since 1873, when German immigrants Adolph Coors and Jacob Schueler arrived and started a brewery. When prohibition began in 1920, Adolph was forced to dump nearly 20,000 gallons of beer into Clear Creek, but just down the street his friend Henry "Heinie" Foss sold Coors beer—and 100-proof bourbon whiskey, available with prescription—at his drugstore, strictly for medicinal purposes. These days, when you drive down Main Street, you're still met with an arch that stretches from one side of the street to the other with *Howdy Folks! Welcome to Golden* in loopy script. And then, in smaller letters, capitalized for emphasis: Where the West Lives. People like to say there are no strangers in Golden.

In the mid-seventies, there were two gas stations. The one where Bundy stopped to fill his tank before picking up Shelley was an old Sinclair station just off the main drag. Even today there's a friendly, emerald-green Brontosaurus on the sign.

Volkswagen Bugs were popular then, representing a kind of post-1960s philosophy of peace and love and freedom, and they held up well as you banged them up and down those back-mountain roads. Mine was cherry red with a rainbow in the back window and a small ski rack on top. *Snug as a bug in a rug.* My Bug was my symbol of freedom—freedom from my parents, freedom from my adolescence, freedom from the suffocating sense of invisibility I'd felt in high school. I paid for it in cash, having saved up months of tips from waiting tables. That Bug was a volte-face from the car I'd learned to drive on: my grandfather's 1963 Rambler with a stick shift and a windshield clouded with cigarette smoke. I loved and loathed that car until the day my grandfather paid a guy $50 to take it away. "We're selling it for a song," he told me.

Ted Bundy learned to drive on a Rambler, too. It belonged to his mother. Years later, in a prison interview, he said it embarrassed him to drive a car so common, so pedestrian, so uncool. He was ashamed to be seen in it. What he had really wanted was a VW Bug.

Just like me.

That was the summer David Bowie's "Golden Years" filled the air: "Look at that sky, life's begun / Nights are warm and the days are young." On our second date, Mark and I went to see *Star Wars.* We stood in line for hours, me in my long jean skirt and hair in braids, Mark in his Levi's with a leather belt and a well-worn buckle with a mountain on it. Soon I started spending nights at his place, a tiny one-bedroom house that once had been a ticket office for the railroad. At the end of the summer, I went back to college and Mark took a job at a hardware store. He played guitar Thursday nights at The Denver Folklore Center, and I would drive down in my Bug to sit in the back row and watch as he sang, played, and laughed with the crowd. In person, Mark was quiet and withdrawn; on stage, he came alive. He was twenty-three, four years older than me, and right off the bat, he wanted to get married. Lots of kids and a picket fence, he said. His family was splintered—his parents had divorced, his two older brothers had moved away, and always there was the one thing— his sister's murder—they couldn't talk about. His mother, Roberta, still lived in the same house where the kids had grown up, built by Mark's dad decades ago. The day we met, Roberta took my hand in hers and cupped it as if I were her own daughter. Mark's father lived outside of town with his new wife, a woman with orange hair and leopard-pattern pants who poured us tall glasses of red wine and took our photo as we sat on her sofa.

"You and Mark could save this family," Roberta said. At the time, I wasn't sure what she meant.

That summer, life seemed full of contradictions. I felt heady with the promised freedom of women's rights, civil rights, the idea of breaking free from traditional expectations. And yet, in Golden, we were all good girls, nice girls, raised in modest homes in the suburbs. We did well in school. We were polite. Our mothers told us not to raise our voices or question authority. We didn't play sports—jogging was considered a passing fad, and twenty-four-hour fitness centers didn't exist. Title IX was still new. Girls weren't supposed to have muscles. Girls weren't supposed to fight. Girls weren't supposed to strike back. We were cheerleaders, or we sat on the sidelines.

Shelley was a good girl. After graduating from Arvada High School, she spent a year with the United Church of Christ at a mission in Biloxi, Mississippi. She returned to Colorado and studied Spanish at Red Rocks Community College. Her class spent a semester abroad in a Mexican fishing village. Later, Shelley went back to visit the people she knew there. She spent a year working and traveling in Alaska. Mark told me that their mother had encouraged Shelley to travel and experience the world. "You can always come back to your hometown," she had told her.

The newspaper reported that Shelley had had a fight with her boyfriend. He let her out of the car and she was trying to hitchhike home. I don't know if this is true. The same story has been told about more than one Bundy victim.

Many women adored Ted Bundy. During the nine years he spent in prison, he received hundreds of letters each month, mostly from female admirers. Bundy married a woman who numbered among the dozens who showed up at his trials and hearings. They had a daughter, conceived during a forbidden conjugal visit. Bundy's wife eventually ended her contact with him and did not attend his execution. She and her daughter moved away and changed their names.

Sociopaths are opportunists. Studies show that they are unusually perceptive at spotting weakness or vulnerability, particularly in women. They're not afraid to seize the moment. Sometimes it's not the person but the situation: girls sleeping in a sorority house, a child walking home from school, a student on her way to the library for an evening study session.

Bundy was a necrophiliac as well as a sociopath. He liked to place his bodies in locations where he could return again and again. Sometimes he brought makeup and hair products.

I couldn't save Mark's family. I know this now. I couldn't save Shelley, whose brief life had already been forgotten and erased by the town, by the media, by the nation. I couldn't save Mark's father, a blue-collar man who worked hard all his life and had to bear sorrows no man should have to bear. I couldn't save Mark's mother, who for years left Shelley's bedroom untouched.

It turns out I couldn't even save Mark.

Colorado is famous for letting Ted Bundy escape. Twice.

A year after Shelley disappeared, Bundy was being held, pending charges for a separate murder, in the Garfield County jail in Glenwood Springs. He was transferred to the Pitkin County Courthouse in nearby Aspen for a preliminary hearing on June 7, 1977. Bundy, a former law student, asked for permission—granted by the judge— to act as his own attorney, thereby excusing him from wearing leg shackles and handcuffs.

One day, while the court was in recess, Bundy asked to visit the courthouse law library on the pretense of researching his defense. As soon as the guard left him alone, he slipped behind a bookcase, opened a window, and jumped two stories to the grass below. A passerby noticed but did nothing; when she entered the courthouse, she asked, very politely, "Is it common for people to jump out of courthouse windows?"

By then Bundy had pulled off an outer layer of clothing and was walking openly down the streets of Aspen, a town like Golden but with more money, higher mountains, and movie stars. He had sprained his right ankle in the fall and walked with a limp. He heard that roadblocks had been set up around town, so he hiked up Aspen Mountain, famous for its ski slopes but now covered in wildflowers, and broke into a hunting cabin near the summit, where he took food, clothes, and a rifle. He set out for the nearby town of Crested Butte but got lost in the woods along the way. After three days on the run, still in pain from the ankle, he broke into a camping trailer, stole more food and a ski parka, and started hiking downhill. Eventually, he found himself at the edge of the Aspen Golf Course. He hotwired a car. Two police officers pulled him over and arrested him when they noticed a vehicle driving erratically down the road.

Bundy had been on the run for six days.

Six months later, back in jail in Glenwood Springs, he engineered another escape. With the help of friends inside and out, he obtained a hacksaw blade, $500, and a floor plan of the jail building. For weeks, each evening while his cellmates showered, he patiently sawed a one-foot square between the steel bars in the ceiling of his cell. He stopped eating and lost thirty-five pounds. On December 20, 1977, with most of the jail's staff on Christmas break, Bundy piled books and legal files under the blanket on his bed in the shape of a sleeping body. Then he climbed up through the hole and into the crawlspace above and dropped down into the apartment of the chief jailer, who happened to be out spending the evening with his wife. Bundy changed into the jailer's street clothes and walked straight out the front door. Once again, he hotwired a car, but it broke down on eastbound I-70. A friendly driver gave him a ride to Vail, where he caught a bus to Denver and boarded a flight to Chicago. By the time the guards discovered the disguise in his bed seventeen hours later, the plane had landed. Bundy was gone.

More than six weeks passed before he was caught. He traveled from Chicago to Michigan, and then took a bus to Tallahassee, posing as a student at Florida State University and renting a room in a boarding house. On January 15, 1978, Bundy murdered Margaret Bowman and Lisa Levy while they were sleeping in their beds at the Chi Omega sorority house. He then stole a van from the university and began driving. On February 9, Kimberly Leach went missing from her junior high school in Lake City. Police tried to trace Bundy's route through receipts from stolen credit cards as he stopped for gas and food. Sometimes he drove a pickup truck, sometimes a VW Bug. On February 15 in Pensacola, he was pulled over, once again for erratic driving, and arrested. He was at the wheel of a stolen VW Bug.

Two months later, Kimberly Leach's body—sexually assaulted, beaten, and decomposed—was found under a collapsed hog shed. Like Bundy's other victims, she was pretty and had long hair parted in the middle. She was 12.

Many girls tried to talk their way out of it. In a police interview, Bundy described what happened when eighteen-year-old Georgann Hawkins started talking. "One of the things that make it a little bit difficult is that . . . she was quite lucid, talking about things. It's not funny, but it's odd the kinds of things people will say under those circumstances. And she said that she had a Spanish test the next day, and she thought that I had taken her to help tutor her for her Spanish test. It's kind of an odd thing to say." He paused, then continued with practicalities. "The long and short of it is that I again knocked her unconscious, strangled her, and drug her about ten yards into the small grove of trees."

He showed no remorse.

My mother, whose own marriage had been disastrous, counseled me to marry and settle down. I loved Mark, but I wasn't ready for that white picket fence. I wanted to finish college and see the world, make something of myself. Still, I didn't want to lose him. He was kind and gentle, certainly one of the most altruistic people I've ever met. My childhood and adolescence had been a roller coaster of family crisis, and he seemed like a safe shelter from the storm. But I was only nineteen. "I'll wait for you," he said. "Please wait for me." So, we agreed to marry someday and saw each other on weekends and holidays. We spent time with each other's families. Roberta encouraged me to be a writer. Mark's stepmother said I should learn how to cook, and began to plan wedding invitations.

One girl, raped and left for dead, did manage to get away, although luck played an extraordinary role. Rhonda Stapley, a twenty-one-year-old pharmacy student at the University of Utah, was waiting at a bus stop when a man in a white VW Bug pulled over and offered her a lift. She thought he was cute, and when she climbed in, he was kind and polite. "He didn't talk much," she said, "but when he did, his voice was confident, his conversation articulate." They drove awhile, and then he turned up a mountain road and stopped in a secluded area next to a rushing stream. He shut off the engine. He wanted to kiss her. "I didn't want to kiss him," she said. "But I didn't know how to get out of the situation without embarrassing myself by making a fuss."

When Rhonda regained consciousness, she was lying on the ground next to the Bug while Bundy busied himself on the other side, organizing the items he generally carried in his back seat: a lug wrench, twine, duct tape, a large knife in a wood case, a meat cleaver, and crutches, which he sometimes used to fake an injury. Her jeans were around her ankles and she couldn't rise or run, so she rolled away from the car. She fell into the stream. As the water carried her over rocks and branches, she kicked off her jeans and crawled out, bruised, naked, and alive, several miles downstream.

We all hitchhiked. We trusted strangers. We believed in the general goodness of all things. Once, when all of us four kids were packed in the back seat of the station wagon and fighting like alley cats, my mother pulled over to the side of the road. "Stop it!" she demanded. "I can't drive!" We giggled together in open rebellion. "If you can't sit quietly," my mother said, "you'll have to walk home."

"Fine," my younger sister said. She got out. She was twelve. "I'll see you at home," she said.

My mother drove off. Ten minutes later, she circled back, but my sister was gone. Two more hours passed before she showed up late for dinner, smirking a little, pleased as punch. I burned with envy at her independent spirit.

Shelley Robertson disappeared on Monday, June 29, 1975. In late August, two engineering students went hiking near Berthoud Pass, in the mountains just outside Golden. They found Shelley's nude, decomposing body in a mineshaft, still bound with duct tape. Little else is known about her death.

My VW Bug frequently overheated, forcing me to pull over to the side of the road and wait. Sometimes it refused even to start. One afternoon, I planned to drive to Denver to meet my mother for dinner. The Bug was lifeless; the starter clicked and then fell silent. I hiked out to the highway and put out my thumb. It was a hot, dry day, and the sun shone in that bright, direct way that is particular to Colorado. It felt good on my face. I remember being thirsty. I often carried a warm Coke in my backpack, but this day, I had only my purse—leather with fringe—with a couple of dollars inside. Rush-hour traffic hadn't started yet, and only a few cars whizzed by. Finally, just as I was ready to give up and head back to my apartment, a sedan slowed and pulled over. A Ford Galaxie, pale yellow with cream seats. The driver looked to be in his early forties, well dressed, perhaps on his way back to his office. He reached over and opened the door from the inside.

"Where you headed?" he asked.

"Arvada," I said. It was an hour's drive.

"Hop in," he said. "I'm headed that direction."

He had long slender fingers, and they tapped the wheel as he pulled back onto the highway. After a few minutes, he reached over and locked my door, as if this was something he always did. He didn't seem to want to talk, so I sat in silence. We drove for about twenty minutes, and then he turned off on an exit.

"Where are we going?" I asked.

"The back roads," he said. "Less traffic."

But there was almost no traffic, and the highway was a straight shot. There was no reason to take a back road. I nearly said this aloud, and suddenly I realized this had nothing to do with traffic. We turned onto a single-lane road, going very fast. I looked out the window at the fields racing by. Then he put his right hand on my left knee. His grip tightened. It was hard to believe this was happening. I thought of Shelley. I thought about opening the door and jumping out. In my horseback riding lessons, I had learned how to tuck and roll, and I thought I might be able to roll off the pavement onto the shoulder of the road. But the side of the highway whizzed by in a blur. The man was silent, his face expressionless. My mouth went dry. I felt lightheaded, disconnected from my body, my heart thudding and my tongue thick.

I started talking. "Where are you from?" I asked. "What's your name?"

He didn't answer. He looked serious. Furious.

"My name is Kris," I said. "I have two sisters and a brother. We have a dog named Pug. I take riding lessons on Thursday nights. My horse's name is Sassy."

He didn't look at me.

I was talking too fast.

"One sister plays the flute," I said, "and the other is a gymnast. My little brother likes to play jokes on his sisters. But we always get him back."

It sounded so stupid. He kept his hand tight on my knee.

I willed myself to stop shaking. I made myself slow down, keeping my voice low and calm.

"I have a boyfriend named Mark, who plays guitar and likes to go rock climbing," I said. "He's tall with brown hair and hazel eyes. He's not sure about college. I have to study tonight for chemistry. It's my worst subject. I thought I would be a veterinarian, but I'm not sure I can pass chemistry."

There was no response. He kept his eyes on the road.

I told him about my best friend from high school who'd just gotten engaged. "I'm going to be her maid of honor," I said. "I've never been a maid of honor, and it makes me nervous."

I told him my mother was waiting to have dinner with me when she got off her shift at the nursing home. She loved being a nurse, but the hours were long. We'd probably order Cobb salads and chardonnay.

I wondered if he was scared, too. His grip on my thigh grew so tight it hurt.

"I might change majors. I think I want to be a writer," I said. "Maybe someday."

The air in the car grew hot and clammy. I thought I might faint. I couldn't think of anything else to say.

But then he jerked to the side of the road and braked in a spray of gravel.

"Get out," he said. "Get. Out."

I fell sprawling out of the car and tumbled down the embankment. I heard the door slam. I lay with my cheek in the dirt until the car roared off. I waited until I couldn't hear it anymore, and then I waited a little longer. It took me four hours to reach a gas station. I stayed down in the gully, walking through the weeds and soft sand and water. Every time a car passed, I huddled down. At the gas station, I used a pay phone to call my mother to come pick me up.

I didn't tell her what happened. I never told anyone what happened. I felt guilty and dirty. I felt it was my fault.

I never hitchhiked again.

Why did the man with slender fingers let me out of the car?

Perhaps it was because I told him the details of my life. My dog, my mother, my boyfriend.

Maybe it was God, maybe it was fate, maybe it was extraordinary luck.

Or maybe he was just an opportunist who lost his nerve.

In his final hours, Bundy called his mother, Louise, twice at her home in Tacoma, Washington. "He kept saying how sorry he was, that there was 'another part of me that people didn't know,'" she said, adding that he sounded "very much at peace with himself." At the end of the second call, she told him, "You'll always be my precious son."

One afternoon, a sunny Saturday in October when Mark and I had been together for over a year, he went rock climbing with a friend. Mark had climbed for years, in Colorado and Mexico, and he and his friend Gary decided to drive up to a popular climbing spot in Boulder Canyon to practice rappelling. A rope slipped, and a piton pulled from the face of the rock. I was taking a meditation class at church that evening when my mother called the church office to pull me out of class. "Come home," she said. She made me sit down at the kitchen table before she gave me the news.

Mark had been living in a small apartment on 34th Avenue in Denver. He was twenty-four. Two days after his death, his brother Rick took me to the apartment. It was tidy, untouched, a half-full coffee cup on the table. We went upstairs to the bedroom and Rick told me to take whatever I'd like to have. I froze at the door. On the tousled bed was a teddy bear I had given Mark as a Valentine's present, a kind of joke. He liked to hike. He liked the mountains. He liked bears.

I still have that bear.

Fourteen years after Shelley died, in the hours before his execution, Bundy confessed to dozens of murders. He had delayed his appointment with the electric chair for nine years and 277 days, and he thought he might delay it a little more. He provided concrete, specific evidence of the murders of sixteen women and admitted to involvement in at least thirty others in Colorado, Utah, Washington, and Florida. The final tally, which will never be known, is at least seventy and likely over 100. The youngest proven victim was twelve, although he was strongly suspected in the killing of an eight-year-old. The oldest was twenty-six. Most were eighteen or nineteen.

Bundy seemed desperate in his last-minute deluge of details, talking fast like some of his victims must have done. He listed names, places, his particular methods of murder. He described the look women get in their eyes just as they die. It was an intimate moment, he said. Previously, he admitted to murdering Shelley Robertson but refused to provide details. It was the only acknowledged murder he wouldn't talk about. Even he seemed to shudder at the memory.

Bundy's final interview was with James Dobson, a preacher who, in 1977, founded the Christian conservative organization Focus on the Family. Bundy hoped Dobson would stay his execution once again, while Dobson hoped a taped interview with Bundy would help with fundraising. With Dobson's prompting, Bundy changed his story and agreed with Dobson that pornography had been the root of his violent behavior. It went all the way back to the 1940s, Bundy embellished, when as a boy he'd found lurid comic books and detective novels in neighborhood garbage bins that featured women being tortured and killed. The interview did not prolong Bundy's life, but Dobson used it to fill his organization's coffers.

On the day of Bundy's execution, January 24, 1989, hundreds of people gathered across the street from the Florida State Prison in Starke. In addition to receiving the death penalty for the 1978 sexual slaying of the twelve-year-old girl, Bundy was convicted of murdering the two sorority sisters at Florida State University. Fraternity boys stood in groups, wearing hand-lettered T-shirts: "Bundy BBQ," "Roast in Peace," "Hey Ted, This Buzz Is for You," and "Bundy World Tour: Sold Out!" Other gatherers banged on frying pans and chanted "Burn, Bundy, burn!" A few people sang songs they had written about him, including one to the tune of "On Top of Old Smokey." A few feet away, several dozen death-penalty opponents stood silently, some praying and holding lighted candles.

At 7:16 am, a journalist left the Q Wing of Florida State Prison, raised his hands, and waved a white flag, the sign that Bundy was dead. The crowd cheered. The hearse carrying the body was held up by traffic that jammed the road.

Some of those in the crowd were parents of victims. "I feel kind of numb in a way," one woman said. "My daughter's murderer was taken care of. He paid for what he did." But she still felt unsatisfied. "It seems like I was sentenced to a lifetime of waiting. Now there's really nothing to wait for."

Roberta Robertson also stood in that crowd, in the row of candle-holders. "Killing Ted Bundy won't make me feel better and it won't bring back Shelley," she told a journalist. "A lot of people seem to want it out of a vengeance. But it gives people a false sense of security. And it's terribly expensive."

Shelley was twenty-four when she died. Mark was twenty-four when he died. I lived to see twenty-four, and thirty-four, and forty-four, and more. More than thirty years have passed since these events. Yet I am still haunted by the image of the man who would have been my husband and the woman who might have been my sister-in-law. My ghost husband, my ghost sister. Why did I get to live, and they did not?

The day Bundy died, he showered, had his head and lower right leg shaved, and then put on dark blue pants and a light blue shirt. He wore manacles on each wrist. Two correctional officers escorted him to the death chamber, where twenty-four witnesses were waiting. He sat down in the electric chair. The officers placed straps over his arms, leg, waist, and chest, with a final strap over his chin and a metal cap on his head. He was asked if he had any last words. "Give my love to my family and friends," he said. A black veil was placed over his face.

Many years later, I saw Roberta at the drugstore. We had lost touch, and she didn't recognize me. She was paying for some small item with coins from a zippered purse. Her face was deeply lined and her hair gray. Her clothes could have been ten years old, maybe twenty, maybe more—a pair of blue corduroy pants and a sweater too large for her small frame, just as I remembered. She pushed the coins around on the counter, exchanged some pleasant words with the clerk, and shuffled out. I wondered if she was still living in the same house. I wondered if Shelley's clothes were still hanging in the closet, and if Mark's hiking boots were still in the hall.

I thought of tapping her shoulder and saying hello. I considered what I might say. She had lost two children. Roberta's grief had seemed so intimate and profound that my words could only have been painfully trivial. Even then, I still carried Mark's death like a knife in my gut. I had learned that you don't get over grief like that; you just learn to carry it inside and try to live with it.

I watched her walk out the door, and I have regretted the moment ever since.

Maybe this essay is about Roberta. Maybe it's about just getting up, day after day, year after year, and not giving in to the grief of the world.

I sold that VW, not long after Bundy got caught for the last time. Like my old Rambler, it went for a song. The tires were bald, the engine dead, the rainbow in the back window faded to a pale ribbon of pink. I pocketed the crumpled $100 bill from the buyer and watched a tow truck take it down the street.

Roberta was ninety-two years old when she died. I read in the newspaper that she had recently written a play which was produced in the local theater. She was working on a second one, a family drama, at the time of her death. The manuscript has been lost.

LORI OSTLUND

The Bus Driver

There were thirty-two of us that first day, standing in a sloppy circle as Miss Lindskoog spoke of cubby holes and taking turns, none of us doubting that we would soon become friends. We were children after all. Children like other children. Over the next thirteen years, Jane and I became—and remained—best friends, *unlikely* best friends, our friendship determined less by shared interests than by proximity, which is how it is in small towns. In 1983, we graduated, Jane barely receiving her diploma, while I finished at the top of our class, a predilection for academics just one of many traits we did not share. Among the few traits we did share was a love of animals, yet within weeks of graduation, Jane began working full-time at the chicken factory outside of town.

I do not want to overstate the degree to which I—back then—might have been troubled by her job, by what some would call her cruelty or hypocrisy, criticism more reflective of the world I inhabit now, a world in which people have the luxury of dwelling on such things. To be fair, I probably viewed the nature of her job in terms of us—as the first step in our growing apart. The next step came with my departure for college that fall, albeit to a state school just two hours away, where the other students felt familiar because we came from the same farming communities and small towns and because we were the ones who left. The group I found myself drawn to was wild, though I was not. I was the quiet one who sat just outside the craziness, watching the others dance, drunk and high, drawn to them not because I sensed some similar wildness inside myself but because I was curious to know what people looked like when they set inhibitions aside. Until then, I had known only inhibition.

Jane and I did not see each other again until the spring of my senior year, when I spent a long weekend at my parents' house. Something—simple guilt perhaps—had returned me there, to this place that I no longer considered home, dropped off on a Thursday evening by a friend on his way to the Twin Cities. Two nights later, Saturday, I found myself desperate to go out, trapped by a former life that was suddenly too close at hand, present in the way that my mother expected my assistance with dinner while my brothers sat idly on the sofa waiting to eat, in the way that my parents had greeted me, my father asking from the recliner as he lowered his newspaper an inch or two, "Is that Clare?" My mother answering from the kitchen, "It's Clare"—each, from a distance and with a cursory nod of their heads, welcoming me home.

Or maybe I fled that night out of simple boredom, ran from the sight of my family huddled around some detective show, my mother asking constant questions about the most basic plot points, my father predictably absent. He took no pleasure in family time. I later found him in the basement, planting seedling cups. My father kept a large garden that, like the universe, expanded just a bit more each year and provided steady justification for his not spending time with us. When I appeared before him that night, requesting his car keys so that I might drive into town to the municipal liquor store—half package sales, half dive bar—my father looked up from his trays of dirt and shook his head no. He disapproved of the liquor store and did not want people to see his car there, but when I promised that I would park in front of his hardware store one street over and walk up the alley to the muni, he reached into his pocket with his muddy fingers and produced the key, for when it came down to it, my father cared most about being left alone. In this way, we were alike.

I had never been inside the liquor store, and when I opened the door that night, I stood for a moment embracing the unknown. The front room, where I entered, consisted of the bar, one pool table, and a jukebox, in front of which, punching in selections, stood Jane. I had received periodic updates on her from my parents, though they reported only on what had gone wrong in her life, a considerable list. I hoped that there were also things that had gone right, but had no way of knowing, for we had not kept in touch those three-and-a-half years. In the beginning, I tried. My first fall away, I sent three letters. All went unanswered. Perhaps the act of penning a letter felt too much like being back in school, like homework, or maybe she had simply recognized the futility of our friendship sooner than I.

"Howdy," she said when I approached her, and I said hello back.

She was dressed oddly—oddly for Minnesota, that is, oddly for our town—in a cowboy hat and boots, a shirt with snap buttons that strained at her stomach. It was the first time I had seen her carry weight. We did not hug. She did not ask about college—what I was studying, whether I liked it, what I planned to do with what I was learning. I did not expect her to.

"I've got kids," she said straight off, her Minnesota accent undercut by something vaguely Texan. "I'm at the chicken factory. Still."

There had always been something childlike about Jane, but that night I could see that she was an adult, someone who snapped necks and paid bills, snapped necks *in order to* pay bills.

"I heard you'd become a mother," I said.

As soon as I said it, it sounded wrong, this talk of *becoming* a mother, as if motherhood were something she had aspired to, when the reality was this: she'd gotten pregnant, twice, and as a result had two girls under the age of three, who, according to my parents, her parents were raising. I wondered, but did not ask, who the fathers were.

Did I feel superior to her as we stood that night regarding each other from our divergent lives? I do recall thinking as I looked at her—twenty-one years old with two children and a mundane job—that only I had a future, for the whole point of the future was that it was unknown, and everything about her life seemed already determined. I recall thinking, too, what a relief my life seemed by contrast. Was I wrong to acknowledge wanting none of *that* for myself?

She went back to punching numbers into the jukebox, and a song began, something country, which was all she'd ever listened to. "I recognize this song," I said. In truth, it sounded to me like every other country song. "Who is it again?"

She snorted. "Conway Twitty," she said, and I nodded solemnly as if to say, "Ah, yes, Conway Twitty."

"So," she said. "I've got quarters on the table."

It took me a moment to understand that she meant the pool table, that she was inviting me to play. "Sure," I said. "Okay."

"I'll gut you like a chicken," she said, still in that strange Texas-Minnesota accent. There was something in her tone, but when I turned to look at her, she laughed.

"I'm not great at pool," I said.

"So you don't want to play?" She sounded neither disappointed nor relieved.

"I'm just warning you," I said, though really, I was filling the silence. The Jane I knew had talked incessantly, but the one before me, this new Jane with two children and a softening waist, did not speak at all, not as she corralled the balls and assessed the cues for warping, nor as she chalked the one that met with her approval, an action that called attention to her hands, which looked strong and capable and like the hands of someone twice our age.

"How's your father?" I asked.

She snorted, presumably at my word choice, "father" instead of "dad."

"He's still got the buses," she said.

"Tell him I said hello. I always liked him."

"Yut," she said, agreeing to tell him or acknowledging my fondness, maybe both. "Break?"

"You go ahead," I said, and she positioned herself at the head of the table, bent low, and, with one hard jerk, sent the cue ball exploding into the others.

• • •

As a kid, I spent a lot of time at Jane's house, in part because her parents were nothing like mine. They drank alcohol, which mine did not, and from a very early age, eleven or twelve, they let us drink with them. There was a part of me that felt I had the best of two worlds: parents who knew that it was inappropriate for a child to drink, a friend's parents who let me do so anyway. To this day, I remain drawn to fun and excess in others, wary of it in myself.

On the night of our high school graduation, Jane's parents threw a party just for us, the class of 1983. They lived outside of town, far from streetlights, the nearest neighbors half a mile away, and so there was a shared sense that the night truly belonged to us, that the rest of the world did not fully exist. Jane's father owned the buses that served our school, which he kept in a large shed constructed for that purpose, but that night he had moved two of the buses outside to make room for dancing, and for the keg and the garbage can half full of punch that left some of the sloppier drinkers with red mustaches. Most of us roamed the property, some playing horseshoes drunkenly in the dark, others sitting in the yard, also drunkenly, wondering aloud how it was possible that we had even reached this point, from which we were now being flung outward.

Miriam, the woman I've now been with for nine years, finds it *odd* that Jane's parents hosted such a party, though such parties—keggers—were not uncommon where I grew up. Miriam was raised in New York, having wine at dinner with her parents, who were both from Europe and considered the American attitude toward drinking puritanical, so what shocks her is not that parents allowed us to drink but that they allowed us to get into our cars and drive home afterward, a position with which I agree, now that I have learned how to view my childhood through Miriam's eyes.

Around midnight, I sought refuge in one of the two unberthed buses, settling in the seat halfway back on the left that, until then,

Jane and I had considered ours. Soon I heard someone on the steps, Jane's father, whom I liked but did not know well, despite the hours I spent at their house. In fact, I thought of him mainly in terms of this bus—the back of his head and his benign, steady presence as he drove. That night, however, he did not settle into the driver's seat but instead came down the aisle and sat across from me and, eventually, began to talk, and then, to sob. I knew that this was the result of alcohol, but because I was not really an adult, despite the way he spoke to me, I did not yet know that one did not cry because they were drinking but because drinking made them think about the very things they were drinking to forget.

"I should have done something," he said, then, softly. "I should have killed him."

He did not identify whom he was talking about, nor did I ask, our shared knowledge implicit in the silence that ensued, during which he sniffled and drank some more from a bottle that only then did he offer to me. It tasted awful, but I drank from it again and again because I did not know what to say to a grown man who was weeping.

"I'm glad you're leaving here," he said at last. By then, he had stopped crying. "You can always come back, but the older you get, the harder it is to leave."

I did not say that I planned never to come back. There in the dark, I just nodded. At some point, he added, "You've been a good friend to Jane all these years," and I stood and got off the bus rather than saying what I felt to be true, which was that I had not been a good friend at all.

• • •

Jane was athletic. I was not, but for a brief period in my early teens I had wanted desperately to play basketball, not just play it but excel at it. The fall that we entered seventh grade—junior high as it was still called in the late seventies—we both joined the team. The coach, whom the older girls all claimed to find sexy, was a man in his early thirties who had moved to our small town the year before with his wife and baby son. Coach-wise, he was considered a catch, for in addition to girls' basketball, he oversaw football in the fall and track in the spring, racking up an impressive record of wins his first year. In his spare time, he taught fourth grade.

A couple of weeks into the season—his second, my first—he lined us up at the beginning of practice one day to run sprints, then paused and took the whistle from his mouth. "Ladies, I've been reading some research," he said, "and it seems one of the best ways to strengthen chest muscles is to run without a bra." His voice sounded the way it did when he explained backspin or zone defense, and then he announced that we had five minutes, in case we needed to return to the locker room. I don't recall whether we all went. I think most of us did. We were serious about basketball, serious about winning—games as well as the coach's praise—and so I imagine that we gladly went and shed our bras, lined up, and waited for his whistle. I do recall that later some of the older girls complained, not to the coach or even in front of him, but in the locker room afterward. "My breasts hurt like hell," they said, holding their bare breasts aloft in their hands, like offerings, to relieve the ache.

Jane and I changed directly back into our school clothes and went out into the late afternoon darkness, onto the after-sports bus that was parked at the curb. Jane's father was at the wheel. As usual, I greeted him and Jane ignored him, and we made our way back to our seat, where we huddled our sweaty bodies together, shivering.

"Did you see it?" she whispered.

"What?" I said.

"His wiener."

We still used words like *wiener*, still found wieners funny. She giggled. I did not, though I had seen it, the polyester of his maroon track pants tented at his crotch as he whistled and we ran, the assistant coach standing to the side, looking elsewhere.

When I told Miriam this story, she said, "And he didn't say any-thing?" and I said, "Who?" and she said, "The assistant coach. How could he just stand there?"

One of the things that drew me to Miriam was her ability to see justice in very simple terms: when something was wrong, it needed to be called out, remedied. It was why she had become a lawyer. Miriam rarely got tired of arguing a point. It was what made her a good lawyer. It was what made her exhausting to live with.

"The assistant coach was a woman," I said.

"A woman?" she said. "Now I'm even madder."

"Why?" I said. It was not that I didn't understand her anger. "Why are men always let off the hook? She wasn't the one telling us to run braless?"

"I'm not letting anyone off the hook. I just don't understand how a woman, in particular, could let something like that happen."

"She was young," I said. "It was her first year at the school, her first job." It had also been her last year, though we did not even know she was leaving until she was gone.

"You're making excuses," Miriam said, "for something that's inexcusable."

I said nothing. It *was* inexcusable. Still, I could not help but wonder whether I might have responded similarly, might also have turned away, that is, and focused—as she, the assistant coach, finally did—on the cart of basketballs in the corner, on the straightforward task of picking them up, one by one, and squeezing, as if to assess their firmness.

I did not tell Miriam that I wondered this. I knew what she would say. "What are you talking about? You would have stopped him."

"People like to discuss hypotheticals," I would reply. "We like to sit on a barstool and lay claim, with unwavering confidence, to our bravest selves. But really, there's no way to know what I would have done, what I would do." Then, I would say what I always said when we found ourselves engaged in some version of this debate: "I mean, look at how many people talk about how they would have hidden Jews, how few people actually hid Jews."

"That's because most people are weak," Miriam always replied, she who had actually lost family members because this statement was true. "You're not afraid. You would have hidden Jews."

I wanted to tell her that I *was* afraid. I was afraid all the time, of not doing the right thing, of not even recognizing what the right thing was, afraid of how hard it was to be in love with someone who always believed the best of you.

• • •

The affair began several months into the basketball season, though, to be clear, I never considered it an affair. *Affair* implies two adults having sex and a victim who is neither of them, though, of course, Jane did not consider herself a victim. She felt lucky, chosen. At first, I did not even believe her when she said they had had sex. It was not just that I was the sort of child who believed in adults, in their infallibility. It was also that I knew Jane, knew she was not always honest, that she was prone to exaggeration.

Then, one night, our telephone rang. It was Jane's mother. "Oh, you're home?" she said, clearly surprised to find me there.

"I just got home," I said, lying instinctively.

"And Jane?" she said. "I didn't think it would be so late, not on a school night."

"She should be home soon," I said, hanging up before she could reply because how could I elaborate when I did not even know what I was lying about? Almost immediately the phone rang again, and I picked it up, fearing that it would be Jane's mother again.

"My mother might call," a voice whispered. It was Jane.

"She already did," I whispered back. "Where are you?"

"With *him*," she said. "At his friend's cabin. What did you say?"

"I lied," I said. "I told her you'd be home soon, but I didn't even know where you were supposed to be, where *we* were supposed to be."

"We're out having pizza with the team," she said, giggling.

The next day at practice, when the coach blew his whistle and we lined up to run sprints, he said that we were going to do things a little differently. "What I'm going to do," he said, "is I'm going to pick the slowest girl on the team and give her a head start, and anyone who doesn't pass her before she finishes, well, that person runs extra sprints."

Whenever he wanted to call someone out—for blowing an easy shot or missing practice—he threw a ball, hard and without warning, enjoying the thump as it hit the girl's chest or back, her startled cry of surprise and pain, and that afternoon, he pivoted and flicked a ball at me. I caught it, then stepped up to the line, set the ball down, and waited for his whistle.

That day, nobody caught me, nobody even came close. As I stood back at the line, bent over and trying not to vomit, the coach flicked another ball, which ricocheted off my shoulder. "Run like that more often," he yelled, "and you might lose a few pounds."

He blew angrily into his whistle, and the rest of the team lined up and ran ten more sprints.

After practice, as Jane and I sat on the cold, dark bus waiting for the others, I blurted out, "He hates me, and now everyone else does too."

"He doesn't hate you," she said, her voice low. "He knows you're my best friend. He knows you cover for me."

"Wait," I said. "Did you tell him I know about—you know, the two of you?"

"I had to."

"Why?" My voice rose, and Jane's fist rose reflexively, landing a quick blow to my shoulder, right where the coach's ball had hit.

"Shh," she said, nodding her head toward her father. Then, "He heard me on the phone with you last night. He asked if you knew."

Thus began the slippery slope of my own complicity. Over the next year, with me as their occasional accomplice, the two of them continued to meet, mainly at his house on the evenings that his wife attended Weight Watchers. His wife was not fat, at most carried a few pounds left over from the pregnancy, as women do, so her participation in this organization perplexed me. I did not yet understand the way that decisions about women's bodies were made, the way that other people, men, tended to chime in, asserting their own wishes. "She's a cow," Jane declared on the bus one day—the regular bus right after school because basketball season had ended—and I knew that she was talking about his wife. When I did not respond, she added, "Who'd want to have sex with someone with such huge, gross tits anyway."

"I hate that word," I said, as though "tits" were the only part of the sentiment I found objectionable, and on the seat beside me, Jane began to cry.

"Well, I hate my body," she said, and she began pummeling her breasts, which had only recently begun to bud. "He's going to leave me." *Leave?* I thought.

"He likes breasts," I said, making my voice consoling because Jane was my best friend after all. "Don't you remember when we ran with our bras off? He got a hard-on."

Jane laughed, a laugh that embraced the change in terminology; we were thirteen by then, no longer giggly girls who used *wiener*. No longer girls with girls' bodies.

• • •

Jane wanted to win at pool—more precisely, she wanted to beat *me*—whereas I was torn: part of me wanted to let her win, while the other part knew that doing so would be one more betrayal.

I won.

Jane threw her cue onto the table and put on her coat, and I followed her into the cool March night.

"Where are you parked?" I asked, as if we were two old friends ending our evening with easy chatter.

Jane did not answer, instead turned in her cowboy boots toward the grain elevator lot, where people often parked even though parking was never an issue, and I went in the opposite direction, across the street and into the alley that ran down to my parents' hardware store. I imagined Jane getting into the same temperamental pickup that she'd driven in high school and driving home to a tiny room where her two children were not, but there, my imagination stalled, for I had no idea what this room might look like, whether her daughters' absence was a relief or a steady sorrow, whether there was someone there waiting, perhaps the man who was the progenitor.

Jane was following me. I sensed it first, then heard the clack of her boots and turned. "Do you have pictures of the girls?" I asked, mainly for something to say.

"They're with my folks."

"The pictures?" I said.

"The girls," she said, an edge to her voice. "They live with my folks. They're better off with them."

"I thought you might have pictures," I said. "That's all."

Throughout much of my childhood, this alley had been home to a stray ginger cat that I courted tirelessly, spending hours talking to it while it regarded me with disinterest. Then, one day it brushed casually against my leg, a small gesture on its part yet so hard-earned on mine.

"Remember the orange cat that lived back here?" I said to Jane.

"I hate cats," she replied without much conviction.

"No you don't."

"I've learned to hate them," she clarified. "You're not the only one who's learned things."

"Of course not."

"Of course not," she parroted, and we began walking again.

"How about your brother?" I asked after a moment.

"Works at the bowling alley in Evansville," she said.

We reached the back wall of my parents' hardware store, and with one quick move, she had me up against it. "It was you," she said. "You reported us." She reached into her jacket, and I saw the flash of a blade.

I recognized the knife, the *kind* of knife, that is. My parents sold knives like it, knives meant to gut fish or flay the skin from a deer. I imagined Jane coming in with the money she had earned snapping chicken necks to buy this knife from my parents, one violence begetting the means for the next, for this knife pressed to my throat.

I had betrayed her. I had told someone about their relationship. I had done the thing that seemed right and necessary, and, in doing so, betrayed her. In college, where I was an English major, I was learning about such things—paradox, irony—grateful to have such words at my disposal, feeling, I suppose, as one does when, after slipping on a pair of glasses for the first time, the world unblurs. But did *irony* even apply in situations like this, situations far removed from the worlds of the kind of people who invented words and assigned them meanings.

Mr. Tesky, the guidance counselor, was a new addition to the school, a man who came in twice a week, mainly to help seniors enlist in the army or apply to trade school or college, a man wholly unprepared, that is, for me to sit down in the closet he had been given as an office and tell him that the basketball coach had spent the last year having sex with my friend. I had made the appointment earlier, so by the time I appeared at his closet door that day, he had probably realized that I was only in eighth grade. Had he thought it odd, a thirteen-year-old making an appointment when she was years away from a future?

"Does it feel weird to have no windows?" I asked, stalling.

He looked around, then laughed. "I hadn't thought about it," he said.

The adult me believes that this should have been a red flag—what good could come from confiding in a person so unquestioning of his surroundings—but the me I was then blurted out, "My friend pukes a lot." When he did not respond, I said, "The coach puts his wiener inside her."

I imagine now—not without sympathy—how the encounter must have felt to him, how he had thought that his job was to sit in a windowless room two days a week handing out forms to disinterested teenagers. Was it his fault that he did not know how to take the story that I was trying to tell: about a coach who slept with a girl, a child, for an entire year, dumping her when she began to menstruate, how she began excusing herself from class, returning with glassy eyes and the smell of vomit on her breath, her spine rising from her back in a strange new topography, and how I, her friend, had done nothing.

The guidance counselor stared at the windowless walls. He did not ask, "Who is your friend?" He did not say, "Tell me what happened." What he said was, "You'd better get back to class."

Two days later as I sat in science class listening to the teacher explain that gas was made up of particles and giggling with the other students because we were children after all—amused by adults speaking of "gas"—I received a note summoning me back to Mr. Tesky's closet. His door was open, and I went in and sat down.

"I spoke to the principal about what you—about your visit," he said.

I looked down. I knew that the coach and the principal were friends.

Mr. Tesky coughed and, in a tone that sounded oddly formal, announced, "The principal has informed me that he and the coach went out fishing yesterday and they had a chat, and he has told the coach to keep it in his pants."

It was only years later that I understood that this—Mr. Tesky's parroting of the principal's casual vulgarity—was an admission of anger. There was nothing more to be done. That was what he was telling me. Mr. Tesky looked away, at the spot where he perhaps only then understood a window should be.

"Why did you do it?" Jane said, the blade tingling against my throat. "You were my friend. You were supposed to help me."

"I was helping you," I said.

"The counselor called our house," she said. "He wanted my parents to come in."

This, I had not known. "Is that how they found out?" I said.

"They never found out. I told them Tesky canceled the meeting."

I did not correct her, did not describe her father's sobbing on the bus the night we graduated or the way that he had spoken, as men often do, in simple, violent terms: *I should have killed him.*

"We were going to get back together," she said. "But you wrecked it. You didn't want me to be happy."

"Of course I wanted you to be happy," I said. "You were my best friend."

"You were jealous."

"Jealous?" I said. "I hated him." I did not spell it out, so obvious seemed the logic of my hatred: he had taken a child whose body and innocence and trust were, to him, sexual, destroyed each of those parts, then continued on with his life.

"You hated him because I loved him," she said.

"What?" I said.

She leaned in close, her breath sour with beer, and for a single heartbeat I thought that she was going to kiss me. Did I want her to? No. The realization came so swiftly that I clung to it—throughout my twenties—as proof that I did not desire women at all when the truth, of course, was that I did not desire her.

She yanked the knife from my throat. "You're a fucking dyke," she announced and walked away—boots clicking—down the alley.

• • •

That was the last time I saw Jane. She was already pregnant that night, with her third child, another girl; this, I would learn from my parents, as well as of the fourth, born years later just before Jane went to prison for turning her poultry blade on a coworker. Somewhere along the way, I came to terms with desire, *mine*, and was living far away from that town when I learned of her sentence—three years, the coworker had not died—from a newspaper clipping sent by my parents, who considered it their duty to keep me apprised of the ways that my former best friend's life continued to go wrong.

A couple of years passed, then another clipping arrived, this one technically not about Jane, unless you were the kind of person who read between the lines, which my parents were not. They were the kind who took headlines at face value—"Popular Coach Dies Tragically, Run Over by Bus"—never questioning "popular" or even "tragically." The driver of the bus—it probably goes without saying—was Jane's father.

The newspaper article mainly reported his version of what happened: that it was dark, nearly nine o'clock, and they'd just returned from an away game, which they'd won. He heard the girls cheering, still, as they ran from the bus into the school to stow their uniforms and call their parents. The coach had gone in with them. Jane's father was sure of that, so when he heard the thud and felt the back wheel rise up, he imagined he'd backed into a snowbank. He drove forward then stepped out and saw him there, pinned beneath the wheel of the school bus.

"The man coached my daughter." That was how the article ended, the reporter framing the statement as an expression of remorse.

No charges were pending.

When Miriam got home that evening, I showed her the article, covering up the text beneath the photographs of the two men involved—coach and bus driver—and asked her to guess which was which, who was perpetrator and who, victim.

She waved the paper away. "You need to call the police," she said.

"What police?" I said.

"In your hometown. You need to tell them about your suspicions. That it might not have been an accident. That Jane's father might have murdered that man."

"I don't know that."

"That's why you need to call," Miriam said in her calm lawyer's voice. "You need to tell them what he told you on the bus that night."

When I did not answer, she asked, "Is there a reason you don't want to call?" She was turned away from me, struggling to open a beer, and I could not tell from her voice alone how she meant the question—conversational or probing. Miriam was not a patient person, but she told me once that when you ask a question in court, you need to be prepared to wait as long as it takes for an answer. Of course, we were not in court. We drank our beers—an evening ritual we both looked forward to, a moment when our days came together, collapsed into one—and still I did not answer.

"The coach ruined his life, too," I said finally. By then, we had eaten dinner and were lying in bed.

"So you do think he did it?" she said, as if hours had not passed.

"Well, he did do it," I said. "But you're wondering whether I think it was intentional?"

"Yes," she said. Her voice was sleepy.

"That's not for me to decide," I said.

"But by not reporting it, you are deciding," she said.

Then, she kissed me and turned over and went right to sleep, confident that I would sleep also, that morning would come and I would wake up and do the right thing, that right things existed, that the world spinning beneath us was a world spinning ever closer to justice.

SUZI Q. SMITH

Get the Water

I keep wiping her forehead with a cold rag, but she doesn't open her eyes, even when I call her name. I whisper songs into her ear and tell her stories, even when Mama says to let her sleep. Seems to me like she's been sleeping long enough. Daddy sent Gordon and Freddy into town to call the doctor, but when they dragged their dusty feet back into the house all disappointed, I knew they hadn't found the doctor at home. Daddy would send them back later that afternoon and again that night, but they wouldn't mind, 'cause it beat sitting around the worried house with everybody's hair standing up and Mama praying in words nobody understands but Jesus.

I walk down to the creek and fill a bucket with fresh water, but the walk feels too long and muddy without my little sister skipping and singing next to me. The sky is all gray and white and still. The patches of overgrown leaves and weeds along the path look like they want to wrap around my ankles and drag me into the brush, where the shadows all have the kind of teeth that bite, so I walk as fast as my feet can carry me, splashing water from the bucket all the way. I wait for Mama's scolding when she sees the pitiful half-bucket of water I set on the kitchen floor, but her hands are twisted up together into horrible knots and she doesn't even see me come in. Daddy is sitting in his chair sometimes, chewing on the end of his pipe and pretending to read, or walking back and forth in front of the piano, muttering. When he calls my brothers to him his voice is sharp and too loud, like a man trying on a new throat without being found out.

I will not sleep tonight, even though Mama finally saw me shifting in the doorway and told me, with all the tenderness of a tired general, to say goodnight to my sister and get myself to bed. I knew it was my fight as much as hers, but I knew better than to say so just then. My brothers' voices roll under the door in marching whispers. I can't hear the words, but I know that the doctor has not come yet. I know that my sister is drowning in her own body. I know that Daddy doesn't know what to do, that none of his books tell him how to pull a lake from a little girl's lungs.

When the doctor comes in the morning, Mama is already wailing. My brothers hang from Daddy's arms and waist, pleading, as he charges the doctor. His voice is a Daddy I have never met, his face the reddest lion. "It is too late," I hear someone shout, "nothing to be done," "nothing, nothing, nothing, too late," all ricocheting around the house like echoing burglars. I try to catch the words with the broom and sweep them out the kitchen door, but I know they will take my sister with them when they go. I let my fingers uncurl from its handle and let it hit the floor with a clack. No one hears it.

Square Dancing

We had gym class in the cafeteria for a week. Ms. Brown said we had to learn how to square dance.	A square dance is a country dance that starts with four pairs facing one another in a square, with the steps and movements shouted out by a caller.	We (we: mostly black kids in the 1980s inner-city) resisted, but she said we had to. We were only in fourth grade and not entirely anchored in our power.	A square is a plane figure with four equal straight sides and four right angles. A square is a body of infantry. To square is to challenge and prepare for battle. To square is to cut into corners.
My mom was a country western dance teacher and in this case could have given me a much-needed gym class edge but this was not a thing to be good at anyway.	Ms. Brown made me dance with Michael Brewer. I did not like Michael Brewer. I did not like Ms. Brown.	When my grandfather raised his fist to my grandmother, she would pretend to pass out. He would rush to her aid, apologizing all the way (as if choreographed).	One time Michael spat on me. I tried to spit back but couldn't get enough weight to it so the spit just dribbled down my lip and onto my shirt.
I raised my hand in every class and was every teacher's pet except Ms. Brown's. It could be argued that I was, myself, a square.	Swing: Man twirls the lady under his arm to finish the swing	My mom met her second husband while she was teaching country western dance and he had a hell of a swing.	This is one of the ways I learned to tell when a boy likes me.
Circle Left: A common call in square dancing, bringing the dancers to join hands and move in a clockwise circle.	No one ever asked me if I liked Michael Brewer. I only knew I did not like to be spat on or pushed down and then be asked to dance.	My daughter told me that when her boyfriend raised his fist, she would pretend to pass out and he would rush to her aid, apologizing all the way (as if choreographed).	Ms. Brown decided we needed to learn to square dance and maybe she was right.

Dark Humor

you know how my hips
have never forgotten the drum?

you know the way my voice
sounds like a conjured Grandmother?

you know how I write
poems like invocations, right?

you know how my spirit never sleeps?
how we laugh at our own temporary blood?

and oh, sweet Lord,
how we laugh!

how buckets of glass leap from our heads, thrown back and open,
how we spill sharp, choking out the swallowed stingers;

how we dance until our feet blister and open,
knowing the stains will tell the story of our movement;

we super magic, we beloved immortal,
even our echoes got knuckles;

listen, in the canyons, over the ocean crashing,
our ancestors stay chanting:

we in here.
we still here.
we been here.
we stay here.
we survived.
we survived.
we survived.

MATHANGI SUBRAMANIAN

Other People's Mistakes

The clinic Alma sends you to is really just the back room of a 7-Eleven across the street from the Thai restaurant where Raj was supposed to propose. There's an examination table covered in last week's *Washington Post* and an ultrasound machine with a cracked screen. The walls are made of cinderblock, and the floor reeks of cheap cleaning fluid and Slurpees. It's not ideal, but you don't complain. You're not in a position to be choosy.

A white man in a leather jacket and ripped jeans butters the ultrasound's plastic wand with gel. When he tells you to relax, your abdomen tightens, and you apologize, take deep breaths, try to will your anxiety away. The man manages to maneuver the wand inside your body, to press it against your cervix. The ultrasound's fluttering screen settles into a single pixelated smudge.

"Well, you're definitely pregnant," he says.

"What about the heartbeat?" you ask.

"Too early for all that," he says, pulling out the wand and cleaning it with a wet wipe. "You need any pills? Procedures?"

Last week, when you went hiking with Alma along the Billy Goat Trail and she made you memorize the address of the clinic, Alma had made you memorize her instructions. And she'd given you more instructions, too.

"Just the test. Nothing else," she'd said softly, allowing the brash currents of the Potomac and the clatter of dry leaves to swallow up her words. "No medications. No prescriptions. No printouts. Get your results and go."

"No thanks," you tell the man, pulling on your black cotton underwear, your sharply pressed Calvin Klein suit pants you bought at Filene's. Patting your still perfect hair, you hand the man a neatly folded stack of bills. You try not to meet his eyes, hoping that your face is one he won't have any reason to remember.

In middle school, your history teacher—a balding white man in tortoiseshell glasses and corduroy pants—waxed poetic about the election of 2016, the appointment of righteous judges, the elimination of funding for reproductive health. When he described how the courts struck down "the bloody legacy of Roe vs. Wade," how they then gutted the legal framework protecting women and immigrants and queer and trans folks, his voice broke with emotion.

Distracted, you stared at your lap, your brown skin smooth with Nivea, your hair sweetened with coconut oil. You were on your period—it was only your second or third one—and you fidgeted anxiously in your hard plastic chair, wondering if the thin maxi pad stuck to your underwear was thick enough to prevent blood from staining your pants. (That day, it wasn't.)

"Missouri was the first state to eradicate abortion clinics," your teacher said. "Shamefully, our home state of Maryland was the last. Imagine what could have been achieved if our leaders had governed with integrity. Imagine the lives that could have been saved. The babies who wouldn't have been lost."

On the smartboard, your teacher projected a photograph of the legislators who wrote the law declaring abortion a felony. They were lined up behind a long wooden desk, their bodies squashed into dark suits, their faces jowly with conviction.

"Heroes," your teacher said. "These men are *heroes*."

Without being called on, Alma called out, "Why are they all white? And all men?"

You squinted at the image, realizing that Alma was right, realizing that you hadn't even noticed. But then again, why would you have? Your whole life, this is the way it had been: white men like these politicians in charge, brown girls like you and Alma doing what you were told. So far, you'd stayed out of trouble. So far, it hadn't bothered you at all.

"Abortion is homicide," he said. But this time, when he spoke, his gaze slid around the room, landing briefly on his cell phone balanced on a stack of ungraded papers, his tablet sticking out of his leather sling bag.

Every electronic device had ears. Some had eyes, too. You knew this because your father constantly reminded you. Because your father feared for your life.

Was your history teacher afraid for his life too?

No, you reasoned, he couldn't be. After all, what did he have to fear? He didn't have a womb.

Just then, the sun emerged from behind a cloud. Hot, fresh light shot through the classroom window, knifing your teacher's shadow onto the wall.

When you leave the clinic, it's only four o'clock, but the light is already fading. Before you start the long walk home, you pause to check, again, that the convenience store looks like nothing more than a convenience store, that you look like nothing more than a customer leaving with a packet of gum in your pocket, an overpriced bottle of juice in your bag. When you cut through the parking lot, you pass a group of teenagers in vintage sweaters perched on the hood of an ancient Toyota, their Slurpee-reddened tongues flashing between their teeth, their bodies reeking of pot and sweat and manufactured cherries. It's a Friday night, and they are loose and gleeful. Their optimism makes your stomach lurch.

You trudge the three chilly miles back to your apartment, unwilling to risk a bus ticket or a metro card. Your cell phone is in your bedroom, generating GPS evidence that you came straight home from work, that you spent the evening in bed, reading a book, perhaps, or sipping a glass of wine. When you finally reach home, it's dark, and your hair smells like wind and woodsmoke and antiseptic. You strip, tossing your gummy underwear into the washing machine alongside your cotton socks, your dusty jeans.

In the shower, you turn the hot water all the way up, erasing the air with steam. Through the half-open window, you can see the alley behind your building lined with forest green dumpsters. Last month, your landlord found an empty packet of Misoprostol fluttering between the trash bags. He called the police, who ribboned off your lobby with caution tape. Like all the other wombed residents of the building, you sat by your door in your best suit, waiting to be interrogated. But before they got to you, they arrested your across-the-way neighbor, a biracial trans man who had once brought a misdelivered water bill to your door. You watched through the peephole as they snapped handcuffs over his sand-brown wrists, as they led him through the carpeted halls to the elevator and, you assume, out the front door.

In the shower, you lean your forehead against the grout. Your abdomen twitches with pain. *Must be anxiety*, you tell yourself. Droplets slither down your limbs, dragging the day into the drain.

You were thirteen when your father gave you "the talk." At school, you'd already sat through two cycles of sex ed, where you'd learned about the importance of abstinence, the reason why abortion was now considered a murder, why women were only allowed to have children within heterosexual wedlock.

"I know about reproductive criminality," you said, prickling with irritation. "Our teachers told us."

"They didn't tell you everything," your father said, his voice barely a whisper. Later, you find out that he powered down all his devices, that he purposely pulled you into a room where the cell signal was weak. "Like, for example, they didn't tell you it's different for you."

"For me?"

"For people *like* you," your father said. "When brown and Black women are accused of reproductive crimes, or taken to courts, you're more likely to be found guilty. To have longer sentences. People like you—I mean, people who look like you—well, what I'm trying to say is, you have it harder."

Self-righteously, you replied, "Who cares? I'm not going to do anything illegal."

"Everyone makes mistakes," your father said.

"Everyone except for me," you replied.

The next day later, your father took you to the post office. He said he had to mail a package, but you didn't see him put one in the car or carry one into the ivy-covered brick building down the street from your two-bedroom apartment. In the lobby, he paused in front of the wall of wanted posters, almost all of them reproductive criminals.

"Take a look," he murmured.

You were a good girl, a rule follower, so you did what he told you. You stared at the rows and rows of stone-faced women, all of them dark skinned, dark haired, all of their images captioned with "Wanted for Murder." Their surnames were Nigerian and Navajo, Mexican and Middle Eastern, Pueblo and Pakistani. They looked like you. They looked like Alma.

They looked like your mother.

Your father's earlier warning broke open like a capsule of poison.

"Did Mom have a wanted poster?" you asked.

"No," your father said. "They didn't need to put one up. They found her at home, waiting to be arrested. You were asleep on her lap."

"Go to a doctor," Alma says. It's Sunday, and the two of you are huddled in your bedroom, door locked, router and devices off. Yellow and orange foliage blaze through cracks in the drawn blinds. You speak in whispers, your breath warm on each other's ears. "A proper doctor."

"There are proper doctors who do this?" you ask.

"Not here," she says. "Overseas."

"India," you say. "I can go to India."

Alma sips the coffee you made her in your Ikea French press, her lips restless on the rim of the mug.

"This is the only option, right?" you ask.

She shrugs and says, "You can wait it out. One in five pregnancies end in miscarriage."

Your window is closed, but the glass isn't thick enough to filter the cacophony of early evening in your neighborhood: dogs barking, children laughing, taxi brakes squealing. Top 40 music pirouettes out of the window of a parked car, its right taillight broken, its exhaust pipe spewing smoke.

When you see it, you automatically think, *What an irresponsible driver.* Until you realize that when it comes to irresponsibility, you are not in a place to criticize anyone.

"You broke up with Raj, right?" Alma asks.

"More like ghosted him," you say. "We haven't talked in weeks."

"Good," Alma says. "Keep it that way."

"Hey Alma?" you ask, your voice barely audible. "How do you know all this? Where to go? What to do?"

"How do you think?" Alma hisses. She stands up so abruptly that she spills the rest of her coffee on your carpet. Instead of apologizing, though, she shoves her way out of your bedroom and heads for the front door.

"It's none of my business! I'm sorry!" you call out, but it's too late. Alma has already tugged on her coat and her shoes, has already slid into the hallway, slamming the door behind her.

Alone, you gulp the rest of your coffee. Its bitterness pools inside you, just north of your womb.

You last met Raj six weeks ago, on your twenty-eighth birthday, at a Thai restaurant halfway between the law firm where he was about to make partner and the educational publishing company where you were a highly valued copyeditor. The waitress seated you in a dimly lit booth with vinyl upholstery. At the cash register, sandalwood smoke rose from a stick of incense and circled a collection of ceramic cats.

Earlier that afternoon, Alma had spotted Raj in a jewelry store. She'd texted you a picture of him leaned over a glass cabinet full of diamond rings. It should have made your heart leap. Instead, your shoulders sagged with relief.

That night, instead of studying the menu, you studied Raj's face. His sculpted cheekbones, his wide nostrils, his cleft chin. You imagined moving into his studio apartment—he would never move into yours—and hanging your suits inside his closet, stretching a fitted sheet across his bed. In a few years, you pictured tossing used baby blankets and stained onesies into his washing machine, retrieving diapers from the top shelf of the closet where he now kept his tennis racket.

Raj waved the waiter over and ordered papaya salad and spring rolls for the table.

"And two Sapporos," he told the waiter.

"Just one," you said quickly. "None for me."

"But you love Sapporo," Raj said. You do not love Sapporo, or any other beer. You'd told Raj this enough times that you no longer had the energy to correct him.

Instead, you fibbed, "I just don't feel like it tonight."

Raj was, above all, a product of his times, a man socialized to believe that women are naïve creatures unfit to govern their own bodies. Every environment Raj passed through reinforced his humanity by dismantling yours. Still, out of all the men you'd dated—journalists and bankers, Black men and brown men, Native men and immigrants—Raj remained the least objectionable. He answered your texts. He never missed a date. On your birthday, he bought you roses. (You prefer hydrangeas, but he didn't know that.) Most importantly, although he wouldn't allow you to fill your birth control prescription—in the last five years, a cis man's signature had become a requirement for accessing the pill—during sex, he wore a condom.

When it came to marriage, Raj was a solid choice. A practical choice. If Raj proposed—*when* Raj proposed—you would say yes.

Saying no would have been a mistake.

After the waiter left, Raj clutched your hand and said, "Listen. There's something we should talk about."

"Yes?" you asked, your pulse racing.

"I really like you," he said. "You're a good girl. And I've had so much fun with you."

"I've had fun with you too," you said. Subtly, you placed your free hand on your lap and squeezed the fabric of your pencil skirt, nervously.

"Which is why this is so hard to say," he said. "I'm really sorry, but I can't see you anymore. This is getting a little too serious, and I'm just not there yet."

"Serious?" you asked. "What do you mean, serious?"

"I mean, we see each other every week. You've left your toothbrush at my house," he said, sighing heavily, as though your dental supplies were a huge burden. "I'm not in a place to have a real relationship now. You get it, right?'

"Oh," you said, your heart sinking, your mind automatically recalculating what it would take to get Raj back, weighing what it would mean to start over, with someone new. "Yes, of course. I get it."

"It's not you," Raj said. "It's me."

At first, you believed him. But then, the next day, you and Alma saw him at a bar with a wire-thin blond woman hanging off of his arm. Her left hand shimmered with the weight of a brand new diamond ring.

After you dig your passport out of your meticulously organized filing cabinet and confirm that your Indian ten-year multiple reentry visa hasn't yet expired, you flip open your laptop and navigate to the airline that you always take to visit your grandmother. At the "destination" dropdown bar, however, you pause, realizing that although you've been to India a handful of times, you've never actually been to an Indian hospital.

Where, in India, is the safest place to get an abortion? Which city will look the least suspicious on your credit card bill? Where can you go without your relatives finding out—without your father finding out—the true purpose of your trip?

Nervously, you enter "medical tourism India" into the search bar, hoping the phrase doesn't tip off whatever surveillance technique the government has instituted to monitor wombed people like you. As the result loads, your phone rings, its screen flashing with a picture of your father grinning into the camera, his glasses halfway down his nose, his mouth folded into a grin.

"Hello Kanna," he says. "Are you free Friday? The temple is having a Deepavali dinner, but Deepak Uncle and Sheela Aunty say they're coming."

"This Friday?" you ask, clicking on a link to a group of hospitals in eastern India. When you realize that they specialize in gastroenterology, you snap the virtual window closed. "Sorry, can't. I've got this work thing."

"Fine. Abandon me then," your father says. Sheela Aunty and Deepak Uncle are extremely conservative. Your father hates dining with them alone.

"I'll make it up to you, I promise," you say, clicking on a page advertising a hospital in Chennai that turns out to specialize in orthopedic surgery.

"What's going on at work?" your father asks.

"We have a—um, a training," you say. It pains you, the lying, the leaving. But if your father knows where you're going, and you somehow get caught, he'd be arrested as an accomplice.

"Hmmm," your father says. In the background, you hear sizzling oil, popping mustard seeds. Your stomach rumbles. "Okay then. How's Raj?"

"Fine," you say nonchalantly. You haven't yet told your father you've broken up. You don't want to hear the disappointment in his voice. To face the consequences of your poor judgement.

As your father rambles on about Raj, you click on a link to a hospital in Mumbai, and then sit up straighter. There, in the corner of the screen, is a link labeled, "Abortions for reproductive refugees."

"All this to say, I believe you have to start discussing your future," your father says. "Have you two discussed marriage?"

"Dad!" you say, bile rising in your throat. You hover your mouse over the hospital link, wishing you could click on it, wishing you could access whatever information it contains, whatever comfort it might provide.

"What?" your father asks. "You've always wanted kids. And, in the United States, you have to be married to a man to have them. Raj would make a fine father, don't you think?"

Suddenly, it's all too much. The lies you've had to tell your family, tell yourself. The hiding and sneaking around. The rejection, the disappointment, the pain. Frustration and anxiety and anger howl through you with a deafening roar and your whole body begins to shake, uncontrollably. Beneath the computer table, your legs quiver, your thighs twitch. Still clenching your mouse, your hands shake so hard they rattle.

They shake so hard, in fact, that, inadvertently, you click on the forbidden link. In an instant, the webpage unfurls on your screen: a banner reading "Abortions for Reproductive Refugees," a series of photos of women smiling from hospital beds, a phone number to call for assistance. Before you can look at it properly, though, it flashes closed, leaving behind a message that reads, "This website is forbidden by the government of the United States of America."

"Shit!" you yell.

"Honey?" your father asks, voice laced with concern. "Are you okay? What happened?"

Your stomach heaves. Your head spins. The afternoon's coffee gushes up your throat.

Without answering your father, you hang up and hurl yourself into the bathroom, vomiting into the sink. As you rinse off your face, cramps crash through your abdomen, wetness seeps between your legs.

When you pull your pants down, your underwear is full of blood.

The day before her sixteenth birthday—and a month before you and Alma started ninth grade—Alma's sister Gabriela held a funeral for her baby. You wore a black polyester dress that left a collar of itchy welts around your neck, a pair of kitten heels your father polished to a dark shine. Throughout the service, which was held at her family church, Alma clutched your sweaty hand.

Instead of reciting some kind of eulogy, the priest gave a sermon about the importance of celibacy before marriage. When he spoke, you couldn't keep your eyes off of the doll-sized coffin displayed on the dais.

"Why is it closed?" you asked. Alma's abuela's funeral had an open casket. You'd been afraid to be in the same room as the body. Alma, on the other hand, had kissed her grandmother's corpse on both cheeks.

"There's no body," Alma said. "Gabriela had a miscarriage. She was nine weeks along. We're only having a funeral because it's the law."

"It is?" you asked. "Since when?"

Rolling her eyes, Alma asked, "Don't you read the newspaper? Like, ever?"

She knew you didn't. Newspapers, you'd told Alma, were for people who didn't have the sense to prevent unwanted pregnancies. People who couldn't control their emotions, their desires. People like Gabriela. Like your mother.

Not people like you.

On the first day of school, Alma arrived at the bus stop alone.

"Where's Gabriela?" you asked.

"In Tamaulipas with my tía," Alma said. "She's finishing high school there."

"What?" you asked. "Why?"

Alma sighed and asked, "Don't you understand anything?"

You run your underwear under the faucet. The blood that runs off of it isn't like your usual menstrual blood, red and clumpy and reeking of iron. This blood is brown, a muddy sludge that reeks of decay. Your period blood smells like life. This blood smells like death.

After you clean yourself up, you pull on a pair of your softest pajamas and massage your most expensive lotion into your skin. Gratitude washes over you. Your body, you think, has saved you. Saved you from committing a crime. Saved you from implicating your loved ones in your mistakes. Under the covers, your muscles unclench, your stomach stills. Exhaustion washes over you.

I'm safe now, you tell yourself. *No one can hurt me. I've done nothing wrong.*

Except that you have done something wrong. The memory washes over you, keeping you awake.

The night you saw Raj walk into a bar with his new fiancée—a woman whose perfect hair matched her perfect skin, whose perfect wardrobe matched her perfect race—you knew you should stay home. Instead, after work, you shimmied into a bright red A-line dress you'd been saving for a special occasion, slathered yourself with French perfume you'd splurged on at duty free, and took yourself out to a bar in downtown DC where the drinks were named after dead white movie stars.

Physically, you coursed with adrenaline. Mentally, you were exhausted. Exhausted from doing everything right. Exhausted from being sensible. Exhausted from the effort of not being your mother. From being yourself.

You paid for your first gin and tonic. A slender, sandy-haired man with hairy knuckles paid for your next three. You don't remember the sound of his voice, the color of his eyes, or his name. You don't remember leaving the bar, or letting yourself into your apartment, or taking off your clothes. Or taking off his.

You do remember the rich, sweet smell of the skin lining his collar bone, the muscles of his back arching beneath your hands. The press of his lips along the perfumed line of your neck.

"A condom," you'd gasped, as he'd run his rough palms between your thighs.

"Don't have one," he'd said, his mouth buried in your navel.

Gasping, you'd pulled open your nightstand drawer and handed him a plastic packet.

"Put it on," you said, seconds before you felt him inside you, before your abdomen rippled with pleasure.

The next morning, you woke up to sore thighs, a headache, an empty bed. And also, to the condom, buried beneath the sheets, still in its wrapper.

You fall asleep just long enough to be startled awake by the wail of police sirens, by red and blue lights renting the bruised purple sky. Three white men pound at your door, fist-falls like bullets. Disoriented, you try to sit up, to pull yourself out of bed. But before you are fully conscious, they have already rammed down your door and burst into your bedroom, they have already raked aside your quilt to reveal your weary body curled in a puddle of blood.

At first, you think there is an intruder, that the police are protecting you. After all, their Kevlar vests, their helmets, the guns strapped to their waists—these couldn't possibly be for you. What would necessitate so much protection? Certainly not a barely awake woman in a studio apartment bleeding through the pajama set she fished out of the bargain bin at Target.

But it *is* for you, all of the equipment and the screaming and the aggression. One of the men—a red head with a crooked nose—snaps your wrists into handcuffs. A blond one with black eyes grips your elbow and says, "You are under arrest for the murder of an unborn child."

The third hovers in the corner of the room, stroking the black stubble on his chin, wondering, you imagine, what to do.

"But I didn't murder anyone," you say, as the blond one hauls you out of bed. "I swear, I didn't. I can explain."

The blond raises his voice and tells you, "You have the right to remain silent."

"Can I at least change my pad?" you ask. Instead of answering, they pull you to your door and gesture to your shoes. You tug on your sneakers and realize, *Of course they won't let me change my pad. My blood is evidence.*

Evidence of the crime I didn't commit.

On the sidewalk, the autumn wind knocks goosebumps onto your forearms. Blood seeps out of your saturated pad, slithers down your thighs. Your tennis shoes squeak against the sidewalk, whining and desperate.

Who was it that betrayed you? Was it the man at the clinic? Alma? Your father? Did the link you clicked send an alert to the police? Or was it a stranger, a neighbor who heard you through the walls, or one of the teenagers in the 7-Eleven parking lot?

In the squad car, your uterus throbs, reminding you that a baby is leaking out of you. You rest your cold hands on the roll of fat above your uterus. Your uterus, which tried to save you. Your uterus, which, you understand now, only has the power to betray you.

As you pull away, you glance up at your apartment building. Curtains slide across glass. Blinds snap, rotate closed. Your neighbors turn away, and you don't blame them.

These days, other people's mistakes are just too heavy to hold.

ERIKA T. WURTH

Candy Francois

There are so many gorgeous photos of me. And I'm beautiful in every one of them; thin, perfect, frozen in time. And the drugs were lovely. They were like ice-skating with your best friend when you were eight, like falling in love, like living on cake. I was in New York for six years in a loft in the West Village when I first met Harry. Harry . . . that womanizing, shitty filmmaker of a man. I had a wonderful life; I lived with a ton of other artists, though I was the only Native American. That made me unique. When I wasn't modeling, I was doing promotional work for clubs (that part was my favorite because they would have us dress up so crazy) but then sometimes I'd get a buckskin gig for a Native magazine and that would be wonderful. I would send a copy to Mom, who would send a copy to Grandma, and they would write me and tell me how beautiful I was but when was I going to settle down? I thought the answer to that was never. Because getting older wasn't real, it wasn't something I ever thought about, it didn't even exist. I was in my early twenties, I was a model, I lived in New York.

I was dating a senator for a while there when I was twenty-two. A fucking senator. He was married. I had to keep it quiet. But the things he bought me. And we did so much blow. My friends loved him, because he would come to our apartment smelling of money and beauty and roll out the expensive drugs and take us all to dinner. And let me tell you how much he loved for me to put on the leather gear I'd gotten from some of those club gigs, and whip his white, white ass. I loved it too. I loved everything about that time. My life was so glamorous and trashy and lovely and I was drunk and high and I felt like a rock star, like I was living inside of a neon light, like I was a god. I was in my early twenties, I was a model, I lived in New York.

The first time I met Harry, I'd just come from a shoot in Paris. I remember walking around that golden city filled with such an intense feeling of euphoria it was sexual; thin, dressed in a Christian Dior suit, my dyed black hair down to my ass, the men in that city practically falling all over themselves for la belle amérindienne and me strutting past and laughing on my way to meet some actor and director friends at a hip new restaurant. I'd been given a bit part in a little film and it was premiering at Red Stick in Santa Fe and I was ecstatic. I was sure that I would make it into film. Much as I loved dressing up for my buckskin gigs, or for powwow or ceremony for that matter, I was happy to play anything. I could pass for a lot of ethnicities. I'd even dyed my hair blond once. And this was my first part in a movie and it had been a long time in coming. I'd been auditioning for years. I'd told myself that struggle was part of it. That it was all about courage, about not giving up. When I'd audition, they'd get this really excited look when I'd come in. But when I'd read, that look would fade and I would leave feeling more and more defeated and depressed every time. I didn't understand. I'd taken a ton of classes at The New School. I figured that modeling was a lot like acting. You had to act when you modeled, you had to have presence. And I did. Everyone said I looked like I was about to go through the camera and eat whoever was on the other side. But modeling had been easy to break into. I told myself that the acting world was more complicated, more competitive. That it was only a matter of time. I was in my early twenties, I was a model, I lived in New York.

I was at a party after the premiere in Santa Fe when one of my friends elbowed me and pointed in the direction of a fat little Navajo guy. *That's Harry Brownhorse,* she said. *And?* I said. *He's a director.* I eyed him and he took it as some kind of cue to come up and start talking to me. I was irritated because I hate it when gross men think that they have the right to hit on me. He asked my name. I asked his, and he shook my hand with one of his wet little paws. He was quick to tell me that his film had premiered at Sundance. His friend Harlen was right behind him and after a while it was clear that those two went around together like a married couple. Later I found out that Harlen's film had premiered at Sundance too. And that it did a lot better than Harry's. Harlen stared at me all bug eyed and silent and drank the PBRs that he'd brought and Harry kept going on and on about how important he was until I became bored. But I knew that I had to play nice, so I acted flirtatious and like what he was saying was entertaining. Though I wanted to strangle his fat little neck when he said something about my friend Sheena being nothing but a pretty little cunt. I'm sure it was because she didn't want to fuck him. He told me that I'd played a really good vampire and his little wife Harlen snorted drink out of his nose and took off toward the bathroom. *Don't mind him*, Harry said and I nodded, though I disliked him even more. I did, however, let him have my phone number right before he left with Harlen as I knew he was a potentially important connection. Harlen had been whining, *Can't we goooo?* in-between gulps of PBR like a six year old nearly all night. Harry texted me for hours. I just kept texting lol back. He seemed to like that. Then I went home with this beautiful Cree actor from Canada who was in another film that was premiering at Red Stick. I wondered the next day if I should have been nicer but after a couple of weeks it was like *fuck that guy* because after the first film, I got another bit part and then later another, both with low-budget Native productions. For a while, I started to believe that things were really happening. But I was never given any lines—or very few. And it kept landing me right back at Red Stick. And Harry was always there. Always trying to fuck me. And I would nod and flirt and text him back and go home with someone beautiful. That's the most humiliating part about it, that for years I brushed him away like he was an insect, like he was something I'd stepped on with one of my

Louboutin heels. Also, I'm Ojibwe and Cree. I practically dwarfed that fucker. And he must have thought I was a moron. I found out pretty quickly that he only did Navajo films, cast Navajo actors. But he liked to find women like me, mixed women, tall women, and indicate that he might cast them, and then fuck them and move onto the next. Please. I'd been using people for years in New York. I knew what it looked like from both sides. If I was going to fuck someone, it was because I was either going to get something from them or because I really actually wanted to fuck them. I was in my early twenties, I was a model, I lived in New York.

One night in New York, after I'd been feeling unusually tired and had just had another audition that I'd obviously blown, I wanted to party. And just my luck, Sheena's boyfriend, who was an executive for Starbucks, was in town and we were all invited to his loft in Manhattan. It was decorated like the inside of a cloud, white and silver. The carpet was thick and soft and bone white and the chandeliers were these strange, lovely things that looked more like sculptures than light fixtures. I was wearing something blue and silky and it was dripping off of me. I sat down on the couch and someone handed me a glass of pinot and I leaned back, my tan arms looking like some sort of precious metal against the white, Italian leather of the couch. People were laughing, and I recognized an actor who I'd just seen in Woody Allen's latest. I took a snort of coke and sipped at the wine and it felt magical, the music coming from the stereo like a dream. I felt invincible, like I was inside one of the chandeliers, like I was pure light. Like I was pure pure. I began to float. I don't remember falling toward the glass table in front of me, my wine glass smashing against it, my nose gushing blood. I don't remember Sheena calling 911 or the ride in the ambulance to the hospital, where I died, twice. I remember waking up in the hospital, talking to the doctor about all of the drugs, the booze, the late nights. I remember Mom flying in from Minneapolis and crying and crying over my bed, my thin, warm white sheets making me feel like a ghost. I couldn't understand it. I was in my early twenties, I was a model, I lived in New York.

Six months later, after Mom had taken me home, after months in a room I hadn't seen for years, after a suicide attempt, after counseling, after several hysterical breakdowns on the part of my mom, I was back at Red Stick, at a party at one of Sheena's friend's houses. He was a buckskin actor. He had been bragging all night about the latest Western he had been in, his long black braids glistening in the light, a joint squeezed in-between the fingers of his left hand. My friend Sheena was flirting with crazy crazy Kes Woodi because she was on shrooms, I was about half a bottle of white wine in, and there was Harry on the other side of the room, a glass of Patrón in his little hand. He didn't recognize me at first. And then when he did, he smiled. I smiled back. My room in New York had been taken over by another model. She was Jamaican. She was eighteen. I had just turned twenty-five. But some friends of mine had hired me to do PR for a documentary and at least I was out of my mother's house. Harry came over and told me I looked hot and I snorted and asked him to refill my wine glass. He did. I drank. I thought about all of the stuff Mom had been filling my head with for the last six months in between feeding and feeding me, about how I wasn't getting any younger, and did I want a baby, and that my modeling days were behind me, and if I got married how I needed to find an enrolled Native because I was just under half and if I had a kid, that kid wouldn't be enrolled unless I did, and that whoever it was better not be a bum like the people I'd lived with in New York. *Where's Harlen?* I asked and it was Harry's turn to snort. I didn't ask. I drank more wine. And he asked me about my life and told me about his latest film, how it was about Indian boarding schools and I told him that my grandma had been to one and about what had happened to her there and then we ended up in a back bedroom and afterwards, I cried and though he pet my arm awkwardly I could feel how desperately he wished he wasn't there. After about an hour in the dark, my eyes wide open, Harry got up and quietly put his clothes on. For a moment I thought he might be pausing to see if my eyes were open or shut but he was only struggling to put on one of his shoes. After I heard the front door close, I got up and wrapped the long, blue sheet around my body and walked through the now deserted living room and opened the front door. I stood at the door for a while, watching his car disappear down the road, into the desert, into the dark. It smelled like rain and I felt sick and twisted inside like a dark, dark, dying gangrenous thing. I closed the door and walked over to the kitchen and pulled a bottle of tequila out of the mess of bottles. There was blood on the counter where a dancer who Harry was going to throw me over for at another party in two weeks had taken the cork out of a wine bottle without a corkscrew and had ended up breaking the bottle and cutting her hand deeply. She had laughed and the men had rushed over to help. I went back over to the couch and sat down with the tequila and drank, hard. I lit up a cigarette and tried to push away the deep, wide darkness that was beginning to fill me. I stared at the empty white walls. There was nothing. My God, six months ago, I was in my early twenties, I was a model, I lived in New York.

PART III

Landscapes

KHADIJAH QUEEN

In the event of an apocalypse, be ready to die

But do also remember galleries, gardens,
herbaria. Repositories of beauty now
ruin to find exquisite—

untidy, untended loveliness of the forsaken,
of dirt-studded & mold-streaked
treasures that no longer belong to anyone

alive, overrunning
& overflowingly unkempt monuments to
the disappeared. Chronicle the heroes & mothers,
artisans who went to the end of the line,

protectors & cowards. Remember
when pain was not to be seen or looked at,
but institutionalized. Invisible, unspoken,

transformed but not really transformed. Covered up
with made-up valor or resilience. Some
people are not worth saving, no one wants

to say, but they say it in judgment. They say it
in looking away. They say it in staying safe in a lane
created by someone afraid of losing ground,

thinking—*I doubt we're much to look at,*
as we swallow what has to hurt until we can sing
sharp as blades. Aiming for the sensational

as we settle for the ordinary, avoiding
evidence of suffering at all costs, & reach
clone-like into the ground as aspen roots, or slide

feet first down a soft slope, wet, cold—but the faith
to fall toward the unseen, against the bleak of most
memory—call it elusive. Call it the fantasy to end

all fantasies, a waiting fatality, the wreck of both
education & habit. Warned inert,
We could watch ourselves, foolish, lose it all.

JENNY SHANK

Hockey Forever, or for as Long as It Lasts

When my son Sam is five, we try soccer. Sam skips around while the opponent, unchallenged, scores. When Sam swims, he sinks. At tennis, he flails. In kid yoga, he clowns. In gymnastics he can't copy the instructor's movements. When Sam is six, I coach his T-ball team. He heaves the ball with a weird sidearm and drags the bat instead of swinging it. He'll learn, I think. But throwing and catching are so hard for him that he's mad. He flings rocks in the outfield and knocks down bats in the dugout. Kids call "*Sam!*" in disgust, the way Jerry Seinfeld used to pronounce the name of Newman, the nefarious postman. I love baseball. But after two seasons, I hang up my coaching hat. I coach my daughter's basketball team too, but I don't even attempt that with Sam. I've seen him try to dribble.

Eventually, after years of searching, we learn Sam has sensory processing disorder of the sensory-seeking type. That means he has to move—run, push, climb, and play—as frequently as possible, or else his self-control disintegrates. Often kids with this type of SPD are athletically accomplished because they are so motivated to practice.

But Sam also has dyspraxia, a lifelong neurological problem that impairs coordination and working memory. The occupational therapist charts his manual coordination at the second percentile, his fine-motor coordination at the third, his body coordination at the fourth. He has trouble following multistep instructions. I always thought he had good balance, but the OT finds that when Sam closes his eyes, he falls over. His proprioception is hampered. He only knows where his body is in space while he's moving. He has to work ten times as hard as other kids just to sit, walk, write, or tie his shoes.

These simple tasks demand intense concentration. But when Sam doesn't get enough exercise, he causes havoc, hitting us and throwing things. Fate relishes a cruel combo. Fine. He plays outside, alone.

One day, a hockey game on TV captures Sam's attention. My husband, Julien, perks up. Hockey was his sport. We take Sam to an ice rink. Sam is fascinated with the Zamboni. He studies its every slow swoop, the ice glistening, refreshed behind it. We sign him up for Learn to Skate. He goes every Saturday, year round. He doesn't tire of it. He asks for a birthday party at the rink and rides the Zamboni like a young Canadian prince. We sign him up for Learn to Play Hockey. He can't follow complicated directions, but he loves to play. Finally, when he's seven, he joins Mites, the youngest level hockey team. Every time we ask if he wants to continue, he says yes. Every day he asks, "Do I have hockey today?"

Sam learns to play hockey in a dingy one-rink facility that looks like it smells like an armpit. The water fountain breaks, and tiles fall from the ceiling. The rink's semipro team usually seems to lose. Expectations are low all around, which always works best for us.

But the year after Sam joins Mites, his hockey club demolishes the armpit rink and celebrates the grand opening of a new facility, modestly titled the Sport Stable. They should have called it the Taj Ma-Hockey.

This immense, gleaming building contains three rinks. Lavish banners emblazoned with the club's every achievement for the past four decades hang above the ice. There are basketball courts, three indoor turf fields, and a weight room, used for something called "dryland training." A big-screen TV blares in the lobby. Smaller screens, mounted everywhere, list locker room and rink assignments. There's a sporting goods store, a coffee shop—the espresso kind!—and a bar. Each of these amenities boasts its own hockey-themed name like *Sticks!* They host "Wine Nights" for "Hockey Moms," the flier for which cracks Sam up every time he reads it. The Zambonis are new here, covered with ads from local merchants, race car style.

Monarch, the Sport Stable's home-ice high school team, immediately wins the state hockey championship when they relocate from the armpit rink, as if channeling the Stable's grandeur. The Sport Stable employs a vast, impressive coaching staff. The director once ran USA Women's Hockey, leading America to two world-championship gold medals and a silver Olympic medal.

When Sam is almost nine, he tries out for Squirts and makes it, just barely. Squirts, the division he's aged into, is more demanding than the Mites. We worry the place is too intense. Five hockey sessions a week seems extravagant, insane. But dyspraxics can't learn without repetition. And when Sam comes home with sweaty hair, I know the evening will unfold gently, free of SPD meltdowns. No other sports appeal to Sam or lie within his range. Hockey is all motion, no waiting.

Only hockey. This, or nothing. With trepidation, we bring Sam to the Taj.

He's a little awkward on the ice. His puck handling lags. He can't always copy the fancy skating moves the coaches demonstrate. Sometimes he holds the stick with just one hand. It takes him forever to learn a crossover. In games, he hangs back, all his aggression dissipated by the Zen of ice gliding. But he can basically do it. He skates and shoots and passes. The exercise strengthens him and regulates his system, like lulling all the bees inside to calm with wafts of smoke.

There are over eighty kids on different Squirt teams at the Sport Stable. We counted when the rosters were posted, to determine how much cover we had. There are three Aidens and a Caden on his team. We should have named him similarly, for camouflage. Still, maybe the coaches don't even know his name and Sam can enjoy his dazey hockey bliss-out in peace, without sticking out as particularly unskilled, making his way to the top of next season's cut list.

As the season starts, Julien asks me if Sam knows what offsides is.

"Sam likes the sensations of hockey," I say. "He doesn't care about the gritty specifics."

I make a practice of trying to understand Sam's sideways brain. Sam likes the ice, freshly glossed. The slide of his skates over the smooth surface. The little curls of ice his blades shave off. The cool air rising off the rink. The cavernous ceiling of the arena. The stick in his hand. The clatter of the pucks and sticks against the ice. The majesty of the Sport Stable. The happy bustle and good vibe there.

When the expensive Boulder Bison jerseys arrive, Julien spreads them out on the carpet in our living room. They are shiny and regal with an embroidered bison patch. Julien ties the laces at the throat, smooths them with his hands. He doesn't even have to speak for me to know what he's thinking. "I would have loved this when I was a kid," he says.

For a moment, each of us silently reflects on his gothic-horror childhood with a schizophrenic mom, which involved no music lessons, sports teams, fancy jerseys, birthday parties, or motherlove.

"It isn't fair," I say.

"If I'd had coaches like Sam's, I would have been a pretty good hockey player."

Julien started hockey at twelve, on a rough-iced indoor rink in New York whose shed-like enclosure was so flimsy that once someone flung a stick and it broke through the siding to reveal the light of day. "I started too late," he says.

"You would have been great," I tell him.

"Sam can't even appreciate this."

"I know," I say. "Aren't we lucky that we can spoil him with things he can't even appreciate?"

As the first game approaches, Julien worries that Sam still might not understand offsides. "If he screws this up, his team will be mad at him, because he'll keep getting penalties."

Julien wants me to show Sam a video because I am the Sam whisperer. Or the closest thing we've got to it. "I coach baseball and basketball," I tell Julien. "I don't know hockey."

"Hockey is really simple. There are only like three rules." Julien looks terrified that the coming game will hold the charlatanry of our parenting up to the light.

I can't convince Sam to watch Julien's video, but I draw a misshapen hockey rink on a piece of paper. Are they oval? In any case, there are three important lines, I think. (There are actually five.) "Look," I say to Sam. "The puck always has to cross this line first, before you can skate past it."

"Okay," he says.

"If the puck leaves this area—" I have no idea what any of the lines are called, so I just point, "You've got to skate out too, or the ref will whistle at you." And your dad will have an aneurysm, I don't add.

"Okay," he says.

The first game comes. Sam's team wins because one kid scores five goals. Sam doesn't do anything spectacular, but he doesn't get called for any penalties. It is a joyful relief.

In the third game, Sam scores a goal. A very Sam sort of goal. Julien witnesses it and texts me. "Sam may have scored. Trying to figure out what happened." Clearly, to the average spectator, it didn't look like your orthodox goal. But I'd be surprised if anything Sam ever does is orthodox. Sure enough, on the team website, Sam's name is credited with a goal. I ask Sam about it.

"I was trying to get out of the way, because I thought Aiden was coming to get the puck," he says, his brown eyes growing wide as he tells me the story. "But he didn't come get the puck. So I just kind of put my stick down, and somehow it went in." Sam is still surprised about how his attempt to flee resulted in a goal.

Getting out of the way is one of Sam's prime survival techniques. He knows his hands don't work as well as the other kids' hands. I have seen him, in a game of dodgeball in which all the other eight-year-olds were boldly vying to catch and throw, instead run, evade, and hide, staying well clear of all the action, until he was the second-to-last kid standing. Because he can't throw well, he can never win, but he can at least delay losing. I like to think he gets this from my grandpa Harry, an infantryman who survived a 120-day span of various battles in World War II in which he was engaged with the enemy for ninety-nine of them. Nazis shot him twice in four days, but he survived.

Later, Sam reads the tag on his jersey and confronts me. "It says OT Sports. Did you put me in an occupational therapy league?"

"No, that's just the brand name. It stands for overtime, probably."

"Look at me," he says. He's watched a video on YouTube about how to tell if people are lying to you. "Your eyes are wide. You're lying."

"I'm not lying. You're on a regular hockey team."

Sam plays four games. The season is underway. We think maybe he can skate through, unnoticed.

One evening after practice, Julien and Sam arrive home and realize that Sam left his new fleece jacket in the locker room. Sam screams. "It's going to be lost! Stolen! I'm never going to get it back!"

Because of his SPD, Sam's nervous system is always cranked to eleven. The slightest derangement of the universe triggers his fight or flight response. When Sam freaks out, he breaks things and throws things. Food hits the floor. Chairs crash. He's ripped a hole in the window screen, broken the fence, trashed a photo he didn't like of him and his sister. After years of effort, he doesn't bite us anymore and hits us less, but his freak-outs are still alarming. The more exercise he gets, the fewer freak-outs occur. We finally learn they aren't personal. And Julien and I will do anything to diffuse them.

Though it's late and he hasn't had dinner, Julien leaves to fetch the jacket. When he returns, I can tell something is wrong. He looks shaken but tells me he'll talk about it later.

When the kids are in bed, Julien whispers the story to me. "I thought the jacket would still be in the locker room, but Coach Jill had it. She asked, 'Are you Sam's dad?' I felt like I was falling."

"So she knows his name," I say. These coaches are good.

Julien nods. "She told me, 'I'm having trouble reaching Sam.'"

This meant she thought he was goofing off. There's always the risk that someone will interpret Sam's slow progress and intermittent attention as insolence or laziness.

"I panicked," Julien says, "but I used my Toastmasters skills." He's been going to club meetings for years and has finally conquered his fear of public speaking. "I tried to tell her about him. Maybe you can email her?"

"Sure," I say. Most adults who interact with Sam eventually turn to me for an explanation of his being.

I Google Jill. She placed fifth in the 1986 US Figure Skating Pairs Championship.

Of course.

She is an expert, a professional. She has the snapping eyes and elfin, tousled haircut of a go-getter. She might not understand us bottom dwellers, clinging to the underside of hockey like barnacles to a swiftly moving ship. I met her once, when I was five minutes late getting Sam from practice. He was trying to be a tough guy but wavering near tears. "He was *really* worried," Jill said, with an alarmed look.

Julien presses his hand to his forehead. "When I was talking to Jill, I felt overwhelmed with sadness and shame."

"I go through that too," I say. "For me it was worst when we found out he couldn't read."

If it's possible for a person to be made of books, then I am made of books. Reading is my love, my profession, my therapy, my life. When I enter a house with no evident books, I'm suspicious of it. I stick close to the exit. So when it looked like reading might not come to Sam, I despaired. I wept. And then I worked. I brought him to specialists and found him a reading tutor. I hired an occupational therapist for his handwriting. I spent hours every day searching for books he might like and reading with him. I took more jobs to pay for it all.

Somehow, I taught him to read.

"The sadness is part of this," I tell Julien, "But you don't need to feel shame. This is nobody's fault. Think of how brave Sam is, to go out there on the ice, when everything is so much harder for him."

"But are we crazy? Signing him up for this elite hockey club?"

"He wanted to do it. He tried out. They let him on the team. We're hurting no one by taking up the last spot on the lowest team."

When Julien reads the email I write to Jill, he cries, even though he rarely cries. I don't know if he remembers how often he told me, when I was crying over the reading thing, that it was going to be okay. Julien had trouble learning to read and nobody even noticed, much less helped him. One day he picked up *The Hobbit* and that was all it took. He painstakingly worked his way through Bilbo Baggins's quest, the sentences making more sense as they accumulated behind him.

Every year we discover some new, basic thing that Sam can't do. He can't open the snack wrappers in his lunch. He can't cut pancakes or carve soap with a knife like the other Cub Scouts. We become grievously alarmed. And then we work on it.

I hug Julien. "Sam doesn't have a terminal illness. He's just terminally Sam. He's doing better than a lot of kids with SPD." SPD often accompanies more serious concerns—autism, chromosome disorders, early onset puberty.

Sam's condition, by contrast, seems almost comic, like a wise guy was sitting around a bar deciding what maladies to dole out and went, "Oh, I've got a good one! This thing where you have a compulsion to play sports but you're no good at them!"

Jill never answers my email, and I take that as a good sign. She's sensitive enough to know something is different about Sam and compassionate enough to want to help him. Still, it's clear we can never hide out among the normals. We will always be caught.

Sam will play hockey for as long as he loves it, for as long as the team lets him, for as long as we're willing to haul him to the Taj five times a week. It won't solve everything. It won't take all the despair away. But when he's on the ice, in motion, Sam's padded legs crouched as he glides, the cool air moving across his neck, he can feel where he is in the universe for once and go quiet inside. So, for a moment, I can rest quiet inside too.

CHRISTINE SNEED

The Last Resort

When we go, it is always very early, and I am never the first one up—it's Mom who lights the fire under the kettle and opens the curtains in the front room overlooking the road and a house the same size and color as ours, but no one lives there since its roof caved in last winter. At this hour, the garbage trucks haven't yet started their trips to the Last Resort, Mom's name for the landfill less than a mile away. It's where she drags me two mornings a week to look for anything she can clean up and sell. The trucks come with trash from all the towns in our county, scattering the crows that pace the ruts, cackling as they inspect the dirt and gravel and us too with their black, curious eyes. The crows flock to the dump in noisy gangs of four and five, pecking at the erupted plastic and paper bags, the smells never bothering them.

When we first get there, I have to tie a bandanna around my nose and mouth and try not to breathe, my eyes watering when the stench of spoiled food is especially bad. Hot days are the worst, but if there isn't much wind, it gets easier after a few minutes—your nose adjusts, which most people don't know because most people don't ever go to the dump. As soon as Mom and I get home, I have to take a shower to get the stink off my skin and hair, but in the summer when I need it most, Mom worries about the well and makes me take a sponge bath if it's been a dry month.

Our house is small—it's only her, me, and Houndstooth, our dog. Most of the time, Dad is an idea, off the grid who knows where—in the Utah desert or on a fishing boat trawling the waters along the California coast or halfway to China on a container ship. He isn't well, Mom admits, and we both know there's more to it than she or I can really understand without him here to explain himself. She also thinks I'm still a little girl, but at seventeen, I already know most everything she doesn't want me to know yet. I've seen our landlord, who is young, not even thirty, looking at me in a way my mother wouldn't like, and sometimes I look back. I write about him and a couple of the boys at school in a spiral notebook I keep inside a box under the bed, in the far corner behind a stack of old math textbooks left over from when Dad taught GED classes in the First Presbyterian basement to high school dropouts—mostly girls who had had babies and kept them, and boys who had left school at fifteen and sixteen to work bad jobs and drink and do drugs until they nearly died or someone close to them did die and they decided it was time to change their lives.

Next fall, I'm leaving here for college, and Mom will have to go to the Last Resort by herself. She will bring Houndstooth, who is six but still acts like a puppy sometimes and will try to eat everything he smells and sees. I don't think it will work to bring him, but she said he'll be her protector—he's a big black mutt, half pit, half German shepherd. She thinks she can train him not to wolf down chicken carcasses and moldy bread and the rotting remains of casseroles.

She knows I'm leaving and doesn't like it, but she also says I need to go. We both know it's most likely me who will be the one to get a good job and move her out of this house with its furnace that spits dust but hardly any heat, and its windows that rattle in their frames, and the floorboards that are so cold in winter you have to wear two pairs of socks, but not your shoes. Dad loves Japanese culture, even though he's never been to Japan (as far as we know), and won't let us wear shoes in the house. Despite the fact he's almost never here, Mom and I have gotten used to going without them.

. . .

On junkyard days, Tuesdays and Fridays, we leave at six, an hour and forty-five minutes before I have to be at school. Most of the time, it is still dark when we get there. Even with the smell, I like the summer best, when the sun is already up, but today is the first day of November, and it is drizzly and cold. Dad hasn't been home in almost four months, and Mom is muttering about divorcing him, which happens whenever he is away for more than a couple of months. Her birthday was last week too, and he didn't call or even send a text, because he only has a Trak phone. There was certainly no card or gift in the mail. She is thirty-nine and wasting her life, she says, on a man she no longer knows.

He sends rent money, but most of the time it's not enough. The house does warm up whenever he is in it, though—Houndstooth thumps his tail against the floor and raises his big anvil of a head each time Dad smiles at him, and Mom cooks from scratch all the things he likes best: baked ham and lasagna and chicken rice soup and cinnamon rolls. When he's gone, she hardly cooks, so unless I do it, what we mostly eat is boxed macaroni and cheese and frozen dinners and salty soups from packets. If I want vegetables, I have to make sure I put them in the shopping cart, which is no longer a problem since most of the time now I'm the one doing the grocery shopping on my way home from school.

We put on scarves and hats and two ratty old sweatshirts each and the rubber boots we found for eleven dollars a pair at a garden center about to go out of business in Germantown, and I check to make sure the thick canvas gloves we always wear to the dump are in the trunk of the car before we take off, Mom saying as little as possible. Last Friday we found a Ziploc bag full of loose change stuffed inside an old running shoe, a few tarnished silver quarters in it along with a bunch of regular quarters and dimes and nickels, and Mom was in a good mood for two days.

Our best finds this fall were a new microwave still in its box, not a nick on it anywhere, a walnut end table with only a few scratches, both of which Mom sold to one of her bosses for two hundred dollars, and a bag full of Easter candy—foil-wrapped chocolate eggs and jellybeans and a few boxes of Peeps, none of it more than a week or two past the expiration date. She let me keep the candy and I gave some of it away at school and kept the rest in my locker. I like looking at it as much as eating it.

When we get to the dump, we park like always next to a chain-link fence with a hole big enough for us to climb through. We have kitchen shears for cutting into promising-looking boxes and bags, and I carry a small shovel and a canvas bag to hold whatever we find. Sometimes it's nothing. Other times it's too big for the bag. We started coming to the dump a couple of years ago, after Mom watched a documentary one night on PBS about people who made a living as trash-pickers.

There's wind this morning with the drizzle. I want to be home, still asleep, but I don't say anything to Mom except, "You look tired. Did you not sleep much again?" She hates it when I say this sort of thing, but my mouth is like a gate I can't remember to close half the time.

She looks at me, her gray eyes flashing behind her glasses. "How nice of you to notice." Even with no makeup on and her hair unwashed, she's pretty. I've noticed that since Dad started disappearing for months at a time a few years ago, not long after my uncle Max, Dad's twin brother, killed himself, she doesn't spend much time making herself even prettier with makeup and perfume. She still puts on a little mascara and eyeliner, but no more lipstick or blush or foundation. Both her bosses at Bachman & Quinn, Certified Public Accountants, have a soft spot for her. She doesn't talk about this, but when I come by the office, I see their eyes grow kinder when they look at her. "They pity me," she says if I tease her about their crushes. "That's all it is." She's wrong but I don't contradict her. They might feel bad for her but they also think she's pretty.

"We shouldn't have bothered coming this morning," I say, a few feet behind her as she heads toward what looks like a fresh pile of trash, some of it busted wooden crates and cardboard boxes with smiling apples on their sides. The Last Resort accepts trash from garbage trucks and from people who come and drop it off themselves, mostly farm families who live in the unincorporated parts of our county. It's these individual drop-offs that are our main targets—their loads are almost never crushed the way truck trash is. When I'm right next to the smiling apples pile, I see there are actual apples in one of the boxes, some of them not in bad shape. I grab six and put them in the canvas sack.

Mom looks at me askance. "They'll be bruised by the time we get home if they aren't already."

"I'll make applesauce."

"You going to eat it?" she says.

I nod. "I'll put cinnamon and sugar in it. Or maybe I can make a pie."

"If you say so," she calls over her shoulder, picking her way through a mound of raggedy Hefty bags, the sticks inside one of them protruding in all directions like porcupine quills.

I can tell she's trying to focus and doesn't want me distracting her with my babble, which is what she calls it when she's tired and grouchy. As the sky starts to lighten, garbage trucks begin to trundle through the gates and noisily drop their loads on top of older, decomposing heaps. I scan the piles before me for small boxes and other dry house trash where dollar bills and coins and clean-ish clothes might be waiting. I start to think about Dad, which mostly I try not to do. He emailed me a week and a half ago and said he was reading F. Scott Fitzgerald's essays and short stories—he hadn't read any Fitzgerald before now other than *The Great Gatsby*, and he said I should read his personal essays, 1920-1940. I checked the library but they didn't have them. I asked the librarian, Mrs. Sayers, and she said she would order them for me but it would probably take a month. I've written to Dad twice now to tell him, but he hasn't written back.

After almost an hour of foraging and coming up with nothing but the few bruised apples and an unopened pack of yellow pencils, I hear Mom cry out.

I look up from the bag I'm picking through—only old papers, candy wrappers, water-stained junk mail and potato peels—and find her about twenty feet away, pulling something out of her boot sole. "I stepped on a fucking nail."

"Did it go into your foot?" I say, my voice too loud, but it's too late. She'll know I'm scared and try to downplay it.

"Not really." She pitches the nail into a mountain of ripped-open bags behind her.

I try to catch her eye, but she doesn't look at me. "When was the last time you had a tetanus shot?"

"It didn't go in that deep," she mutters. "It's not a puncture wound. More like a graze."

"If you haven't had one in ten years, you need to get one."

She turns fully away from me now, but I keep staring at her back until she turns around again. "I'm fine, Trudy. Stop being such a worrywart."

"If you get tetanus—"

"I'm not getting tetanus! Jesus. Don't be such a drama queen."

"And I'm not coming here anymore," I blurt, my eyes suddenly burning with tears.

She opens her mouth but closes it again. We stare at each other for a few seconds before she sighs and walks over to a box that reads *Sunshine Farms*, corncobs and a yellow sun on its sides, stooping down to cut into it. "Fine. Suit yourself," she finally says, pulling out a dirty gray-white towel like the ones at cheap motels. She stuffs it back in the box and stands up, her face tight with disappointment.

"Let's go home," I say. "We're not going to find anything good today."

She glares at me. "Who are you? The Oracle at Delphi?"

I watch her stab into another Sunshine Farms box, this one water-damaged, not sure I want to see what's inside, but I can't force my eyes away, wondering if I meant what I said about not coming back. I'll know for sure on Friday when I hear her waking up and putting on the kettle.

Inside this second box is a heap of what look like gnarled roots attached to papery brown onions. "Flower bulbs," says Mom. "At least that's what they look like to me. I wonder why they got thrown out."

"Someone probably died," I say. "And their family didn't know what else to do with them."

"I knew you'd say that."

"It's probably what happened."

She ignores this and makes her way over to another pile of tattered boxes and two overturned milk crates, what looks to me like books inside. "You don't need to be such a wet blanket," she says, barely loud enough for me to hear.

In fairness to her, it's not that terrible at the Last Resort if we find something good—clothes and shoes with their tags still on them, or a like-new toy or curtains and bed sheets in their store packaging. We found wooden salad bowls last week that must have been used only a few times, if ever. She thinks it's people getting divorces who throw out these expensive things, but I really do think it's the relatives of someone who's died.

She has her theories about everything, not just who would toss out perfectly good bowls and knives and why. If she hadn't married Dad and had me when she should have been finishing college, she'd probably have at least a master's degree in American history, which was her major, or a law degree, which she used to talk about going back for. It's not too late, I tell her. She could go to college with me, but she gives me an annoyed look and says, "Who do you think will pay for that?"

My answer is always the same: "We can get scholarships and loans."

It's what I'm counting on, especially the scholarships. I won't be valedictorian—that'll be Micah Busse, who lives with his grandmother because his mom died when he was three and he doesn't know his dad. He has never once gotten anything less than an A. I've had a couple of Bs, in geometry and advanced algebra. Two days ago, I submitted an early decision application to Dartmouth, and there's probably no way I'll get in because even if I had all As, I doubt I'm good enough for them or any other Ivy League school. What I'm counting on—if I have any chance at all—is the essay, the story about my uncle's suicide and my dad basically losing it and all but leaving my mom to raise me on her own.

"Don't play the pity card," Mom said when I told her what I was writing about. "It's pathetic."

I ignored her. It occurred to me not long ago, watching Mom cry over *Sleepless in Seattle* one Friday night when she'd put it in our dying VCR for the five-hundredth time, that I'm the realist in the family. She believes if you work hard and don't wish other people harm, good things will naturally come your way, but I can already tell that's not how it works. From what I've seen, if you have any kind of advantage, you'd better use it, and my one advantage is my sob story, no part of it a lie, and I'd be an idiot not to let a few other people know about it if it'll help me out.

"Maybe I do need to go to the doctor and have my foot looked at," Mom says, interrupting my thoughts. "What do you think?"

She's limping a little now as she moves toward me. I rush over, nearly tripping on two soggy pizza boxes, and take her arm, steering her in the direction of the car, which isn't very close.

"We need to go. How deep did the nail go in?" I ask, trying not to raise my voice, knowing I'd scare her if I sounded as freaked out as I feel. She could get lockjaw if she hasn't had a tetanus shot since high school.

"Not that deep," she says. "But it kind of hurts."

"You'll be okay, Mom. You probably hit a nerve or something."

She doesn't say anything, and when we get to the car, I drive us to the urgent care clinic that's one town over, which is just opening when we get there. There's only one other person ahead of us, a guy with his hand wrapped in a bloody towel, the blood stains brown, which means he must have cut himself last night. Mom looks queasy when she sees him, and I whisper to her to look away. She whispers back, "We can't afford this."

"Yes, we can. It's your effing foot." I feel as angry as I did earlier at the dump when I told her I wasn't coming with her anymore. I want to yell at her and the guy with the bloody hand and the woman behind the desk. I don't know how we ended up here, so poor Mom has turned us into trash pickers, and for months now, I've been trying not to hate Dad, but sometimes I really do. It's not like I didn't love Uncle Max too, who always wore shorts, even in the winter, because he loved summer so much, who always had a silly joke for me, one it sounded like he'd found on a Popsicle stick, who'd call me on my birthday pretending to be Bugs Bunny or Daffy Duck—up until I was twelve and things started to veer off the tracks for him.

Dad should be here with Mom and me. He doesn't send enough money and he almost never calls, but what could be easier? He could get a real cell phone. He could get antidepressants and talk to a doctor or a therapist. He could be my father again if he tried. Maybe he'll kill himself too, but he should be here so Mom and I can at least have the chance to fail at helping him. Uncle Max wasn't married and didn't have a girlfriend either when he died. He lived alone and I know he was lonely. Dad at least has Mom and me and Houndstooth, but it's like he doesn't even see us.

Mom and I sit down on two green plastic chairs facing the gray-haired woman with long red fingernails who checked us in, and when I put my arm around Mom's shoulders, she starts crying. She does it without making a sound, her body shaking just enough for me to realize what's happening. "I bet you just need the doctor to clean up your foot and give you some antibiotics," I whisper. "You're going to be okay."

She doesn't say anything, doesn't nod or give some other sign she's heard me.

I think of Houndstooth then, who must need to go out, who hasn't had his breakfast yet. If Dad were home, he could feed him and let him outside. If he were home, we wouldn't be here, waiting on someone to look at Mom's foot and make sure she doesn't die of lockjaw or blood poisoning or whatever else people die of when they step on a nail in a landfill. I don't like it when I start thinking this way because I know there's no point to it. Last time he was home, he said he was feeling better and wasn't going to leave us ever again, but three weeks later, he was gone, only the usual note under the flour canister saying he would be in touch, saying he loved us and he was sorry but he needed to get his head on straight again.

Mom ripped this note into dozens of little pieces and threw them out the back door. There was no wind, and the pieces only scattered a few feet away. Some of them were still there in the dirt the last time I looked.

RACHEL WEAVER

Dizzy

Eleven years ago I woke up to find the room spinning. In the soft blue-gray light of morning, the walls folded and slid and picked up speed. I pressed my body hard against the mattress, frantically searching for something to hold on to, but everything was moving with me.

When I'd gone to bed the previous night, I'd felt fine. I had not been drinking. Nothing like this had ever happened to me before.

Closing my eyes, I pushed the covers off slowly and dropped to all fours next to the bed. My only thought was that maybe I could crawl away from the vertigo. The carpet rippled beneath me like the surface of the ocean.

I'd just left a life I loved in Alaska to enroll in a two-year graduate creative-writing program in Colorado. My boyfriend had come along to help with the move. I was supposed to drive him to the bus station in Denver that morning so he could begin the 2,500-mile trek back north without me. Now I wasn't sure I could.

I made it to the bathroom by sliding my shoulder along the wall. I thought if I could just brush my teeth, maybe have some coffee, things would right themselves. I was so wrong.

My boyfriend drove us to the bus station while I sat gripping the seat with one hand, the other splayed out against the passenger door, every muscle tensed. I felt as if I were on a roller coaster after having shotgunned seven beers. I remained at the station long after my boyfriend had thrown his duffel over his shoulder and disappeared into the bus. I stared at the waxed orange-tile floor, watched it start to spin, and tried to figure out how I was going to drive home. Because there was no other option, I slid into the driver's seat, stayed below the speed limit, and somehow didn't puke until I got to my apartment.

Later that day, the first doctor looked in my ears, checked me all over, and declared me healthier than most thirty-one-year-olds. Meanwhile I clung to the exam table and tried not to move my eyes. I'd told her about the recent changes in my life. "Too much stress," she said.

Three months earlier I had been trapped in the elbow of a slow-moving Alaskan river by a seven-hundred-pound brown bear and her three cubs, the banks on either side too steep for me to climb. I had spent forty-five minutes keeping the mother bear in the sight of my rifle—finger on the trigger, safety off—as she'd snapped her jaws, paced, and false charged. Not even a tinge of dizziness that day. "I'm pretty sure it's not just stress," I said.

The second doctor was an ENT—an ear-nose-and-throat special-ist. He cleaned the wax out of my ears and referred me to the third, a physical therapist who specialized in the vestibular system, which controls balance and stabilizes eye movements. The therapist made me lie down, whipped my head to the right and left, and had me roll onto my side for ninety seconds and then sit up quickly. When that made me worse, she did it again.

I had not sustained a blow to the head. It wasn't the altitude; I had lived in Colorado before with no dizziness.

An all-day seasickness had taken hold, with intermittent periods in which the world would whirl at blurring speed, forcing me into a fetal position on my bed, on the floor at Costco, on the sidewalk next to a busy street. A dense fog moved into my brain, making it hard to think. Words slid around on the page, as did cars in their lanes. Computer screens made me sick. So did rocking chairs and people who gesticulated while talking. I was dizzy in my dreams.

I had to wait three weeks to get in to see the fourth doctor, another ENT. She spent fifteen minutes with me, then sent me on my way with a quick "Nothing is wrong with your inner ear."

The dizziness was constant, and the brain fog grew worse. No one knew how to help or even had a name for what was happening. I struggled through every assignment, every class, every day. By the four-month mark I'd dropped down to one class and was hanging tight to the shreds of my original plan.

The fifth doctor told me to stop eating dairy.

The sixth was a neurologist not covered by my insurance. An appointment cost $250, with two fifteen-minute follow-up phone consultations at $50 each and a prescription that cost $400 and kicked me into depression. "Oh, yeah," the doctor said on a third $50 phone call, "depression is a common side effect."

I had to find a full-time job: I needed better insurance and more money to pay for doctors and prescriptions and rent and food, although I was too nauseated to eat much. When interviewing for a job at a lab, I held as still as possible in the chair, hands clasped tightly in my lap, and hoped the interviewer wouldn't notice how I swayed in a wind that wasn't there.

The lab hired me and gave me insurance. Six months into my illness I dropped out of school. Each day I went to work, came home, and slept until I had to get up and do it all over again. I paid endless co-pays, covered all the specialists and tests that my insurance didn't, filled prescriptions, and ate as much as I could keep down. My weight continued to drop until the thickest part of my arm was the elbow. People commented that I looked great. They wished they could get dizzy and drop some unwanted pounds.

The sixth doctor ordered an MRI and extensive blood work and mentioned that it might be a brain tumor or possibly multiple sclerosis, but we wouldn't know until the test results came in.

After several weeks of elevated stress, and therefore elevated dizziness, the results came back negative.

The seventh doctor was an ENT who specialized in dizziness, which seemed promising—except for the framed optical illusions hanging in the hallway outside his office. He answered a text from his wife during the ten-minute intake interview and then ran a test that involved shooting water and air alternately into my ear, which left me too dizzy to function for several days.

The eighth, an ophthalmologist, decided it was a problem with my vision and prescribed eye exercises.

The ninth referred me to the tenth, who was more than an hour late and then was in a hurry.

I took pills and suffered side effects that only one percent of people get—most often a lightheaded dizziness on top of my seasick dizziness (there's a difference), a weird tingling in my arms, shortness of breath, exhaustion, depression, and irritability. I had more blood work, another MRI, and a CAT scan. I had tests done again, just in case they'd missed something the first time. I passed every one. Nothing amiss. A master's degree in writing, my half-written novel, my plans to return to Alaska, and the boyfriend all slipped away, one after the other.

As my former classmates began their second year of graduate school, I began my second year of illness. I was referred to a physical therapist who had a sandbox in her office and seemed in worse shape than I was, but she at least offered me access to the library for the blind.

"I'm going to learn Braille?" I asked.

"They have audiobooks."

Before the dizziness I'd read one or two novels a week and always had a pile by my bed. Now I couldn't make it through two lines before the nausea took over. I longed to escape into a good story and resented everyone I saw engrossed in a book.

Doctors eleven through fourteen were chiropractors. Such violence in their hands.

A man named Dennis answered the phone at the library for the blind. I had a two-page list of novels I wanted.

"Yep, we have that one," he said each time I gave him a title. I heard his fingers tapping keys as he looked up book after book.

"How many can I have at once?" I asked.

"There's no limit."

Everything else had a limit: the number of minutes I could look at a computer screen (four), the number of times a day I could navigate the stairs at home (two), the number of chores I could do in a row (one).

Dennis mailed me an eight-pound audio player and every book on tape I'd asked for. When I pushed the extra-large PLAY button, though, it wasn't the same. I hated it. I wanted to read.

The fifteenth doctor, a primary-care physician who brought her dog to work, told me I should just get used to it.

The sixteenth, a spine doctor, asked if in all my years of competitive gymnastics I had ever landed on my head. He ordered extensive X-rays and then sent in his assistant to tell me I was fine.

A dull headache came on that lasted a year.

The students I'd started graduate school with graduated. The boyfriend bought a commercial fishing boat and got engaged to someone else.

Doctor seventeen said, "If sixteen other doctors have not been able to figure out what's wrong with you, then I won't be able to either."

Doctors eighteen through twenty-six were all the same: a long drive, a long wait, bad magazines, a scale, a nurse, another wait, a doctor focusing on my problem for five or six minutes, and then that nothing-is-coming-to-me look, that I-have-a-lot-of-people-waiting-for-me look, maybe followed by a prescription or two, then one more visit to say the pills hadn't worked, and eventually a slow shake of the head that meant *Don't come back.*

When I talked to my brother and my mother on the phone, I heard worry in their voices, and I saw it on the face of the attractive fireman who had asked me out a few times.

Conceding that I would be a person who listened to books instead of reading them, I pulled the audio player out from under the bed and pushed PLAY.

Doctor twenty-seven ordered another MRI.

Doctor twenty-eight, an acupuncturist, said the wind in my body was blowing in the wrong direction.

I waited an hour and a half to see doctor twenty-nine, an ENT who stayed in the room exactly seven minutes before hitting a button on the wall that summoned her assistant, who whisked in to schedule my next appointment as the doctor whisked out. But I forgave doctor twenty-nine all this because she also said she would not give up on me.

Doctor twenty-nine prescribed a medication that made me dramatically more dizzy, and then another medication that made me pass out and puke, and then another medication that took the edge off the dizziness. Verapamil: the first thing that had helped. I could still barely think through the fog, but the dizziness was decidedly better.

"What does that mean I have?" I asked.

"I have no idea," the doctor said. "Verapamil affects many systems in the body." She referred me to doctors thirty through thirty-two, all vestibular physical therapists, with the understanding that I could come back if none of them had any answers. I was made to stare at a whirling disco ball and stand on an unstable surface for unbearable minutes at a time. The therapists sought to show my brain how to deal with its new baseline. I would learn how to be dizzy in the world.

Another year passed. I taught myself how to hide the dizziness; how to walk down hallways without weaving; how to run my hand along furniture and walls to stay upright in the dark; how to squint one eye just enough to keep the corners of rooms in place. It wasn't possible for me to curl up and quit. I had to keep my job to keep my insurance. Because I could not get fired due to an inability to function, I functioned.

When the fireman got down on one knee, I said, "I can't. I'm too dizzy."

Because I hated the look of pity that people gave me when I mentioned the dizziness, I stopped talking about it altogether.

In the 1980s I had been a competitive gymnast. My coach could be mean, but I got better because of it. He would push me, and in response I would push myself beyond what I thought I could do. Dealing with this illness was no different. I ducked my head and pressed on because there did not seem to be any alternative. I acted normal enough that most people didn't notice. This wasn't new either. When my dad had dropped dead of a heart attack when I was seventeen, I'd learned how to make other people feel okay about it before I'd ever learned how to make myself feel okay about it.

Doctor twenty-nine did not give up on me exactly, but she did retire and move someplace warm.

Doctor thirty-three was fresh from residency training and had taken doctor twenty-nine's place in the practice. He decided I had a vestibular migraine and told me there wasn't anything more to do for it besides take Verapamil, which I was already doing. Then he shrugged, pushed away from me on his rolling stool, and started tapping something into his computer. I decided I did not have a vestibular migraine because, if I did, and this was the best it got, my life was basically over.

That night I suffered my first-ever panic attack.

A few weeks later a physical therapist saw me crying while I was doing the disco-ball exercises, and she suggested doctor thirty-four, an allergist who'd had some luck with chronically dizzy patients. Doctor thirty-four noted my lifelong allergies and thought perhaps elevated histamines were causing swelling in my inner ear.

I took the small white pills he prescribed. Within days, walls stopped shimmying like curtains in the wind. Floors stopped rippling like water. The headache diminished. I did everything else he suggested: I ran the HVAC system in my house on fan only in the middle of summer. I vacuumed and sent a bag of dust to Johns

Hopkins. I filled three more prescriptions and bought a weekly pill container so I would not miss a single dose.

I invited doctor thirty-four to Christmas dinner.

Whole days passed in which I was consumed by how lovely it was to grocery shop without nausea, how nice to drive at night with the windows down past fields of still horses, how good to be able to tip my head back in laughter and not worry that it would leave me reeling with dizziness. I saw relief on the faces of my brother, who had moved to Denver, and the fireman, who had not been scared off.

Three months later the walls began to shimmer ever so slightly. The headache returned, and I was shoved back onto the tossing sea that no one else seemed to know existed. It was worse now, all of it— the dizziness, the fear, the isolation—because I'd had a small taste of freedom. Doctor thirty-four was stumped. The pill combination he had used to fight the dizziness had been overcome by some unknown force. He worked on my case intently for another year while I perfected Achieving Anyway: a state of complete disconnect between how I felt and how I acted.

Because I still dreamed of becoming an author, I had all my textbooks converted to audio and took one class at a time until I finished graduate school. I worked on my novel by memorizing each paragraph and then writing it by hand over and over with my eyes closed until the words were exactly how I wanted them. One paragraph a day. On good days, two. Because the fireman still would not give up on me, we began to plan a wedding. Because I did not want to work in a lab for the rest of my life, I started teaching a writing class here and there.

Doctor thirty-four referred me to an ice cube of a doctor who ordered another MRI, got my hopes up about an unusual surgery on my inner ear that could possibly cure me, but eventually told me there was nothing to do and stared at me with the don't-come-back look.

I sat on the floor in the hallway outside his office and cried. Once I'd composed myself enough to drive home, I noticed a migraine clinic run by a neurologist across the hall. The only diagnosis that had not been completely disproven was vestibular migraine, so I walked in and made an appointment.

In the weeks before the appointment, I held tightly to the hope that a migraine specialist would know of some way to treat a vestibular migraine that doctor thirty-three, the fresh-from-residency-training ENT, hadn't.

The neurologist was even colder than the ice cube. Because I did not see auras or have blinding, painful headaches, she did not think I had migraines. Mostly she was annoyed that I didn't complete every day a long checklist in the headache journal she gave me. The instructions for filling in the boxes were confusing, and the pages swam before my eyes. The neurologist did not want to talk about how I felt; she wanted to pore over the data. When there was no data, there was apparently nothing to talk about.

She was skeptical of the idea that I had a vestibular migraine, but she had a pages-long list of drugs to try, and I transferred my hope to that list. The first few pills she prescribed decreased the dizziness—until the side effects (dizziness, usually) kicked in and made everything worse.

Over the next two years I got mildly better at filling out the daily checklist. I learned that the neurologist was a marathon runner and that patients were not allowed to touch the pamphlets in her exam rooms; if I wanted to look at one, I was to ask either her or the nurse. Every three months, after spending ten minutes with me, she prescribed different pills. Some made the dizziness slightly better, most made it worse, and all gave me side effects that almost no one else gets.

In those two years I mastered Achieving Anyway. Because I still held on to the belief that this problem would someday be solved, the fireman and I started a family. Because I lost more blood delivering our twins than anyone should—and because I couldn't take a full dose of Verapamil while breast-feeding—I fell into a dizzy, exhausted haze that pushed me beyond every physical and mental limit I'd thought I had. Because I had not just one infant but two, I didn't sleep much. Because we were broke (I'd stopped working at the lab), I started a teaching business. Because an agent picked up my novel and wanted me to rewrite it, I rewrote it.

My husband was at the firehouse the night one of our sons woke me up, unable to breathe. He has asthma and needed to get to the emergency room as soon as possible. I picked him up and immediately passed out due to a migraine drug I was taking. Both of us hit the hardwood floor together. I woke to find him struggling for breath, his head on my chest, his face blue. I had no idea how long I'd been out. I grabbed his brother and somehow drove all three of us to the hospital.

A few months later I woke up feeling as though someone had my heart in a vise. I ended up getting an EKG and being told I needed less stress in my life.

When the ten-minute neurologist stayed in the room only ninety seconds to tell me I most likely didn't have migraines at all, but to take this next pill and come back in three months, I began to plan how to end it: the railroad tracks. Late at night. I stopped wearing my seat belt, hoping something would happen that wouldn't be my fault. I pushed away everyone who cared about me. The ten-year mark was approaching, and I was done. It was all I could do to get through each day.

I picked doctor thirty-seven based on the fact that his migraine clinic was close to my house and he didn't sound like a jackass on his website. I sat in his waiting room and stared at the headline "Jennifer Aniston Breaks It Off For Good." Then I followed a medical assistant to a small room, waited some more with my eyes closed, and finally described to doctor thirty-seven my situation in one long, spoken-too-many-times, run-on paragraph. In the ensuing silence a cold fear spread in my chest. If he couldn't help me, I was terrified of what I would do next.

Doctor thirty-seven didn't wear a lab coat. He didn't enter everything I said into a computer while half listening to me. He kept the lights low—which, when you think about it, is considerate when you're treating people who have headaches. He sat still and listened and watched me closely.

"I think you have a vestibular migraine," he finally said.

My vision began to tunnel. This was it. There was nothing anyone could do. This was going to be my life.

He went on to suggest two quick shots that he recommended all the time for vestibular migraine.

I tried to focus on him through the heavy fog of my dizziness and the way the room swayed around him. *All the time?* No one had given me a shot before.

"We can do it right now," he said, "see what happens."

I knew what was going to happen: the dizziness would get worse. I explained that I didn't have a ride home. He watched me: not in a calculating, mind-whirring, get-it-done-and-move-on-to-the-next-room kind of way, but in a human way. "I think it will help you. And if for some reason it makes you worse, we'll make sure you get home."

I was done caring what happened to me. Deciding I could sleep off the effects in my car until I was safe to drive, I agreed to the shots.

The medical assistant administered the injections: sumatriptan and Toradol. I paid the co-pay, made it down the stairs, and sat in my car.

Fifteen minutes later I was staring at the doctor's two-story office building. It held still. My head didn't hurt. The heavy fog was lifting. I felt like an alien to myself. I had forgotten what normal was like. I had forgotten everything except how to survive, and I had been losing my grasp on that. I watched cars drive by and found that tracking their motion did not cause my head to spin. I didn't move, because I was afraid if I did, it would come crashing back. I should cry, I thought. A normal person would have cried with relief, but I was too exhausted to do even that.

The parking lot was directly across the street from the office of a chiropractor I'd seen in year three: ninety dollars a visit twice a week for a full year. I had driven right past doctor thirty-seven and his two shots 208 times.

It's now more than a year later. I still see Dr. Tanner—doctor thirty-seven—twice a week for at least half an hour each time, longer if I need it. We spend that time talking, trying to untangle the knots my malfunctioning nervous system has tied itself in for eleven years. He's got it 80 percent untangled, thanks to Botox injections and twice-a-week sumatriptan and Toradol and a few other migraine drugs whose dosages he is constantly adjusting based on how I'm doing. I have come to understand that some migraines can present with no pain or auras, only dizziness. I have come to understand that migraines are exacerbated by histamines, which is why the allergist was able to make a dent in my symptoms.

I can now read a bedtime story to my boys, the three of us curled up on the couch together. The look in my husband's eye is a little less worried as he watches me navigate my life. More and more people are taking my writing classes. My novel has been published.

There continue to be setbacks in my treatment plan, along with leaps forward—including an entire month in which I barely noticed any dizziness at all. Dr. Tanner steadily attempts to figure it out by not giving up, by not rushing, by asking questions and listening.

I know I'm supposed to say that some good has come of all this, that I appreciate each moment now in a way I didn't before, but that's not the case. Mostly I feel a hot, boiling anger: That the migraine specialist at a major hospital never tried either of the injections that Dr. Tanner gave me on my first visit. That the vast majority of doctors I saw showed no interest in helping me figure out what other avenues to explore when their particular specialty turned out to be a dead end. That I am not unusual; that other people get the same confusing, rushed, non-patient-centered care that I received. That, for many doctors, patients continue to be numbers, billable in seven-to-ten-minute blocks of time.

Dr. Tanner may still one day give me that I-have-no-idea-what-else-to-do look, but that's okay. He's only human, and so am I—a fact he recognized and acted on from the beginning, which has made all the difference.

TARASHEA NESBIT

Sometimes the Floor Needs Swept:
Reckoning with Home

The first time I heard the phrase "flyover country" was in graduate school, in a midwestern city, and the person explaining the phrase was telling me a bit of gossip. A faculty member, it was rumored, might not get tenure, because her book was published on a flyover press.

Flyover? I asked.

It was after a reading from a visiting writer, who wore a velvet blazer, brought to us from a university near a coast, surely, as they often were. I would have had a small plate in my hand of things I'd never eaten before that year: triple cream brie, those thin crackers you spread fancy cheese on, and in my other hand, red wine. My new weekly, free dinner, especially useful at the end of the month, before our stipends came in.

Like in 'flyover country'? she said.

I cocked my head.

She explained.

Not a more prestigious, New York press, but a university press located in the Midwest.

Where I'd lived my first twenty-three years, Ohio, was a place never to land, a place to dismiss for a better elsewhere. I'd wanted to dismiss it, too, as soon as I learned there was an elsewhere. New York was the fixation of my ambition—although how it became that is difficult to place. In high school, I requested college brochures on a dial-up computer connection in my father's unheated den. Barnard was the school I most wanted to go to because I suspected I was queer. But I chose the state school, instead, persuaded by my father not to acquire much in student loans. After graduation, I worked in an optical shop and nearly made the mistake of getting married at twenty-two, before I left for graduate school in St. Louis.

At school, I submitted a poem for workshop with the line, *The floor needs swept.* The famous poet leading the workshop said there was something wrong with that phrase.

Could I read it aloud?

I read it aloud.

Don't you hear that? he asked.

When I showed no recognition of my mistake, he explained. He passed his copy of my poem to me, which had "to be" written between "needs" and "swept." I studied it, considered it, but did not "fix" it. That is how we speak here, in Ohio, if you are from certain regions. Sometimes the floor needs swept.

A year after graduation, a friend and I crossed the west, and on our way to Seattle—the farthest place I could get from my family and still be in this country—I met the person I later married, in a gold mining town in Nevada. We moved to Seattle, then Tacoma, then Denver, then Boulder. Ten years passed. I thought I'd done it; I'd forever outgrown the Midwest.

I got pregnant, I birthed a full-term daughter, who was born unbreathing, we grieved, I published a novel, I finished a PhD, I went on the academic job market, and I was pregnant again. A school in the Ohio Valley of my youth, with a coveted 2-2 teaching load, health insurance, and a 10 percent matching 401K, was hiring. I brought my husband and our five-week-old to the on-campus interview. My husband was surprised that the pizza place did not know what kalamata olives were. I knew this place, these people. I was offered the job.

With a seven-month-old and a western husband that confused the geographic location of Ohio with Illinois, I moved back to the Miami Valley, back to where my entire family—mom, dad, brothers, sisters, cousins, uncles, grandparents—live. I was ecstatic to have a job, but the first year was also a mourning process I did mostly privately, for how unsavory, ungrateful, and insulting it is to tell someone living where you live that you are mourning living there.

That was four and a half years ago. Before I moved back to the Midwest, I'd stopped seeing any good in where I came from, if I ever saw good. I did see good there once. Riding in the back of the pickup on our way to a family reunion at Miller's Grove, that was a good memory, with my closest cousin, Jessica, four years older, as our grandmother drove. Jessica liked to look through our grandmother's large JCPenney's catalogs and pick out items for her future baby's nursery. I liked to pick out business suits I'd wear to my nebulous "professional" job. Jessica died from complications of addiction the year I moved back to Ohio. That is one way to frame it. Or she died from grief, from loneliness, from poverty, from childhood sexual abuse, from a lineage she could not escape, because she was more loyal than I, I sometimes think. Because she wanted and needed her family, I sometimes think, whereas I had worked myself into needing nothing, and left.

A friend I made in Denver flew in from New York City to give a reading. I was apologetic through the cornfields. I asked her which version of mediocre she'd like to have for dinner: Indian, Asian, American.

She laughed.

She loved New York. *It reflects the way I experience life. Messy and chaotic.*

I drove us past the tawny winter fields, the houses on acre lots with man-made ponds, across train tracks, a strip mall.

This place resembles life for me, I told her. *There is nothing and then you die.*

I qualified: *I mean, the distractions are few here from mortality, or at least the distractions that would be most distracting to me: art openings, museums, book launch parties.* Privately, I also think I'm spending more time with my children than I would if I lived elsewhere: we bake muffins, we go to the park, we spend many hours reading books.

There is nothing and then you die, I said, again, lightly, and she laughed.

Given the options for shopping within forty-five miles—a T.J. Maxx, a Walmart, and a Goodwill full of clothes from the T.J. Maxx and Walmart—as well as a busy teaching schedule and two small children, I don't drive into the city (Cincinnati) to shop for clothes, or get my glasses adjusted, or wax my eyebrows, and the clothes I order online are quick purchases, often ill-fitting, and get returned, or linger too long in my closet, unreturned, until I have to keep them because the return period has expired. So, I dress like I'm from here, too—nothing from an independent designer, no whimsical shoe from a boutique on Pike or Pine in Seattle. Those days are, if not gone, dormant, buried beneath the fallen maple leaves of my life. This is how one grows into midwestern, I think, but perhaps this is just how one grows older, making calculations, valuing time over appearance.

A small town asks you to be a little more decent. Our friends who moved here from Brooklyn say they learned quickly not to display road rage—that person you flipped off could easily be the person in front of you in preschool pickup, at the grocery store.

I was writing at the coffee shop when someone put their hands on both my shoulders. I turned to see not a threat, as I had anticipated, but a professor and friend who has started writing personal essays. She has good news: her newest essay will be published soon. We celebrate for a moment and discuss our kids and a visiting scholar's talk—a conversation both of us could be having at any university. My friend was an undergrad at Barnard the years I would have been there. It is entirely possible I would have found myself here, back in the Miami Valley, had I lived those years in New York. I could have ended up exactly where I am. Except if it had happened that way, I might presently owe more money in student loans than we do on our mortgage.

The goal of a teaching job with a 2-2 load in an affordable, reasonably-sized West Coast or mountain town where we have friends, or family, grows fainter and fainter. I like my colleagues and I like the students here. I understand the subtlety; the small cues that suggest a lot more is going on beneath niceness. Our shared geographical upbringing does, more than I thought it would, give us connection, and I have a particular tenderness for students who come from lineages closest to my own. Last week I taught Joan Didion's "Goodbye to All That" and my students said that the essay worries them. They fear they'll one day feel the way the narrator does. Most of them are from this region. We discuss how Didion downplays that leaving New York is also returning to where she is from, California. *It's shameful to return to where you are from*, one student says, and others nod. It's the last thing they want to do right now.

My dad used to say, upon his friends asking about me, my lapsed visits, all the holidays and birthdays I missed, *I knew I raised my daughter right if she never came back.*

Many of my family members are in recovery. The automobile factory my grandfather worked at has closed, and with it, other factories my family members have worked at, and the associated correlations with unemployment and opioid addiction are palpable. But I know that more from my friend who is an ER doctor than how I once did as a child, scared and confused watching a caregiver nod off. My fantasies are no longer to live in a loft in New York—I know what kind of lineage I'd need, or what kind of risk-taker I'd need to be, to live that way. Now my fantasies are that a small cottage adjacent to our house will come on the market, and my mother will buy it, or we'll help her buy it. My mother, who is looking to buy a home again, after losing hers to bankruptcy when I was in college, told my daughter that her ideal home is next door to us and after school, my daughter comes to her house for a snack. I can see the possibility of comfort in this.

On certain spring afternoons though, a Friday after meeting with students, when the sun shines as I bike home, I could admire the crocus and daffodils pushing through hard clay. But often, I wish for a back patio in a city to meet friends in. I wish for a bookstore. I miss watching fiddlehead ferns unfurl along the trails of the Pacific Northwest. I seek a little lapse in being aware of my mortality.

But perhaps there is something else I'm reckoning with here. As a child, ambition was my survival skill. If a parent was shooting up, if a pedophile was calling me, if I knew what bar to call to find my other parent, until I didn't and they were gone for a week—I studied, I practiced basketball, I wrote. I trained my mind to imagine a future where happiness resided. Happiness, I thought, was elsewhere. But elsewhere, it turns out, was not necessarily geography. The pattern of my thinking—when stressed I catapult out of the present and plan the future—was an important survival strategy I'm trying to unwire.

When people ask about my family and I pause too long for social comfort, my husband offers, *She was raised by wolves*. But I don't blame the wolves. Before them were their mothers and fathers, their mothers' mothers and fathers, and to all of them, a lot of hurt, not much money.

I want surprise and delight, I tell my husband when I get home, sulking in a way he has little sympathy for, which is a trait I mostly appreciate about him. We push the strollers to the ice cream shop and stop to watch the tadpoles flitting about in the creek.

I have never called this place flyover country.

The floors need swept, I say sometimes, of this daily mess that is two children eating dinner. I say it if I am tired, if I've forgotten, or if I'm choosing to teasingly offend my husband. I wonder what our two children will say, if they will drop "to be," if they will say "soda" or "pop," what they will choose to identify with, to hide, when they begin to see and hopefully question the implications of these differences. She's done it once, our daughter.

Mom, she said, *my dress needs washed*.

What did you say? her father asked, smiling. He had heard her.

To my surprise, it gave me great delight.

KHADIJAH QUEEN

The Dream Act

CHARACTERS
Note: A maximum of four players play multiple roles. Race, age, gender, and other appearance markers may vary with individual productions at the discretion of director and playwright, and according to resources.

THE BEL CANTO
THE FAIT ACCOMPLI
POSITIVE POLLY

THE DREAM KILLER
THE ANGEL OF CORN
THE SOCIAL DISSERTATIONIST
THE GOOGLE CHAT STATUS

THE COLORATURA
THE CHAIRMAN OF ENTERTAINMENT
THE DREAM ABOUT MISMATCHED SHOES
THE SALTED CARAMEL MOCHA

SOMNIUM EFFIGY
FLESH EFFIGY

SETTING
For scenes 1–3, choose one from one or more of the following: anything from the first act of an Ibsen play, a scene from the fifth chapter in any Octavia Butler novel, or simply a repeating projection of one or all of the following: Graciela Iturbide photographs, still life

images from Neruda's odes, or the mural of ODB in Brooklyn. For the latter, call the setting REPEATED PROJECTION and treat it like a static character in all scenes. Or, let the setting be outer space. Sound: "Mass Appeal" by Gang Starr or the instrumental version of Big Sean's "IDFWU."

SCENE 1

THE BEL CANTO (*slowly, spreading hands and arms open*)
Welcome, sensitive population . . .

THE FAIT ACCOMPLI
Before dawn, the muscles gather to bone and squeeze. It feels like all night rabbit punches.

POSITIVE POLLY (*to the audience*)
Can I tell you something? My physical therapist is the BEST.

THE BEL CANTO (*whispers*)
I have an anxiety disorder. In retrospect, a slow stutter . . .

THE FAIT ACCOMPLI
It feels like a wish for immobility is reasonable. It feels extreme, without the pleasure of falling through air, the aftermath of landing.

POSITIVE POLLY
She applies just enough pressure to loosen those traps.

THE BEL CANTO
And I'm drawing self-portraits in pain, making stump rubbings in an arbitrary fortress ruin . . .

THE FAIT ACCOMPLI
Weaknesses unearned and unwelcome.

THE BEL CANTO
I think in triplicate amazement, tough, subtle, esoteric debauchery
as best mission . . .

THE FAIT ACCOMPLI
Small accumulations, the array of attack dull slaps in miniature
becoming the usual beast—

POSITIVE POLLY
You know what else I love? I love that pressed hair smell. Especially
when you grease it up first.

THE BEL CANTO
. . . all swoon, revoked. *(lowers head, looks at hands)*

THE FAIT ACCOMPLI
I'd like to astonish you with my language, but only in your dreams.

POSITIVE POLLY *(skips offstage)*

(BLACKOUT)

SCENE 2

Sound: "Give Up" by FKA Twigs

THE DREAM KILLER *(in a bootleg, grayscale Technicolor dreamcoat)*
What kind of idiot pays attention to dreams? How can you even
afford that?

THE ANGEL OF CORN *(chewing gum)*
Absurdism is my life. Between the ground of absurd and ism is
where I live.

THE SOCIAL DISSERTATIONIST *(smoking a Black & Mild, paces slowly back and forth the whole time but stops abruptly to deliver lines)*
How can people not be into anti-racist dystopian theories?

THE GOOGLE CHAT STATUS *(throughout, takes baby steps in a square on stage, speaking lines when right behind another character, peeking over their shoulder)*
Something's not right.

THE DREAM KILLER *(snorts)*
Also, and I should know, you're terrible at voguing. *(starts voguing, really well actually)*

THE ANGEL OF CORN *(clearly high on an illegal substance)*
There's an Aryan in my bed speaking Norwish. I'm going to put something Norwish on my body. I think it makes perfect sense.

THE SOCIAL DISSERTATIONIST
Let me advocate for the devil on this one . . . what's really the difference between Miley twerking and my li'l cousin Reggie IV deciding to join the ballet?

THE GOOGLE CHAT STATUS
Trying to reconnect . . .

THE DREAM KILLER
That's hard to believe, given your questionable history of sniffing trash.

THE ANGEL OF CORN *(really convinced)*
In the right context, a tattoo artist would say of course I know Norwish. It's better than a tattoo of corn on your ass. We could be like Camus and do *Waiting for Norwish.*

THE SOCIAL DISSERTATIONIST *(stops pacing)*
And also, some days you just *don't* wanna think about how the rape and enslavement of your ancestors shows up in your facial structure.

THE ANGEL OF CORN *(looks around, confused, scratches head)*

THE GOOGLE CHAT STATUS
Whoops . . .

THE SOCIAL DISSERTATIONIST *(strokes chin)*
How does one astonish a racist? You would actually think it's easy, but *(blows smoke)* not the case. I would tell you about that lady who didn't seem to like how I spread out my books and laptop at the big table in the coffee shop, but if I start listing I could go on forever and ever.

THE ANGEL OF CORN *(frowning, hands on hips)*
Why is there a didgeridoo in the background?

THE GOOGLE CHAT STATUS
Try now.

THE DREAM KILLER *(smiles evilly, opens coat like a flasher, brandishing an array of weapons)*

(BLACKOUT)

SCENE 3

Intro sound, fading as players enter from offstage in ostentatious costumes with great swagger at varied paces: "Mon cœur s'ouvre à ta voix" *by Jessye Norman. They can land anywhere on stage and move around or stand at will.*

THE COLORATURA

Your own abduction in a dream signifies helplessness.

THE CHAIRMAN OF ENTERTAINMENT

You can't con a con man, I heard that in a movie.

THE DREAM ABOUT MISMATCHED SHOES *(nodding, excited)*

In his traveler's mind, the Bulgarians were relevant.

THE SALTED CARAMEL MOCHA *(looking all sexy)*

It's okay if you fetishize me.

THE COLORATURA

If you're holding someone else against their will, let go.

THE CHAIRMAN OF ENTERTAINMENT

I don't have any favorites; I like to say I like them all.

THE DREAM ABOUT MISMATCHED SHOES

He would go from Bulgarians to Papa Smurf.

THE SALTED CARAMEL MOCHA *(continues preening)*

I'm just the right balance of power and sweetness.

THE COLORATURA

Nothing there about how feminism enters the collective unconscious. But, forgetting to reside in the core of grief, you could
learn to knit Fair Isle sweaters for your captor(s).

THE CHAIRMAN OF ENTERTAINMENT

But honestly, I haven't been this bored since the early 1990s so I'm
drawing a blank.

THE DREAM ABOUT MISMATCHED SHOES
   Now that fool is Googling all 54 countries in Africa! *(walks off hurriedly downstage left, shaking head)*

THE SALTED CARAMEL MOCHA *(posing, downstage right)*
   You know you want me. No whip. *(struts across stage, switching hips, until downstage left exit)*

(BLACKOUT)

SCENE 4

SETTING: A clear day, bright blue sky, few clouds; five crows float to a centerline lamppost on a busy street (can be a projection). Elton John's "Believe" plays. Lights fade in on players center stage an arm's length apart. As one talks, the other rhythmically hums, steps like Black fraternities/sororities, or does a Riverdance, but not so loudly as to drown out the other character.

SOMNIUM EFFIGY
   I had a dream last night parts of my body were not my body, not myself.

   My legs went to Harvard. My stretch-marked chest resettled from Iraq. Compton claimed my hands and my shoulders, Cape Cod. I wish I could explain it. But my throat came from the woods of Germany and my mouth spoke only Xhosa.

FLESH EFFIGY
   I dreamed I could find a place for all the places my body had been. My Andalusian hips could sit somewhere with ease and softness, like the texture of dyed silk.

My hair lost all its color. My eyes belonged to the owls. I could fill my belly, more French than Italian, with Petit Verdot and dark roux.

Everything I could smell, though, led me to Korean BBQ kitchens, which means I could be a tourist. But I couldn't lift my arms unless I carried wood from the Brazil nut tree, and only then to make fire, not paper.

I didn't feel lost. I felt off-kilter, disconnected, but I knew (because my brain went back to its beginnings) that I could make myself whole, somewhere.

SOMNIUM EFFIGY and FLESH EFFIGY *(together, holding hands)*
And I wake up as the only thing not burning.

(CURTAIN)

PART IV

Futures

Interview with Young Adult Fiction Authors

Olivia Abtahi, Traci L. Jones, and Denise Vega

Many of the pieces in this anthology speak directly to or about our authors'
younger selves, such as Steven Dunn's piece on his experiences with reading
during his K–12 education, Lori Ostlund's piece on high school sexual
abuse, and Addie Tsai's essay on familial violence. In considering notions of
future in relation to stories and storytelling, it seems poignant to include an
interview with YA fiction authors to get their take on how issues of social
justice impact young adults, and how concepts of equity and social change
enter their work.

INTERVIEWEES

OLIVIA ABTAHI'S debut YA novel, *Perfectly Parvin* (2021), received
the SCBWI Golden Kite Honor, a YALSA Odyssey Honor, and
numerous starred reviews. Her sophomore novel, *Azar on Fire*, was
published in August 2022, and her middle grade novel, *Twin Flames*,
comes out in 2024.

TRACI L. JONES'S debut YA novel, *Standing Against the Wind* (2006),
won the Coretta Scott King/John Steptoe New Talent Award. Her
additional titles include *Finding My Place* (2010), *Silhouetted by the
Blue* (2011) and *Ransoming the Captive* (2022).

DENISE VEGA is the award-winning author of seven books for kids
from toddler to teen, including the YA novel *Rock On* (2012) and
the award-winning picture book *If Your Monster Won't Go to Bed*
(2017).

This anthology centers on social justice issues. As YA authors, you speak directly to younger generations, who are also our future leaders. What kind of messaging do you hope to convey to them through your writing? Do you hope to educate them? Validate their feelings and experiences? Inspire them? Prompt them to take action? Provide hope? Perhaps something else?

JONES: I try not to be heavy-handed in my thematic goals within my writing. I think this generation of teen readers is more savvy and has more world knowledge than past generations. The best I can hope for is to highlight and validate their feelings and experiences. If they feel inspired to action by reading my writing, that is a huge and unexpected bonus for me.

VEGA: My biggest goal is to do my best to reflect and validate their feelings and experiences. Like everyone, teens need and deserve to have books that mirror their own experiences, but I would also like to provide hope in what can often feel like a dismal and hopeless world as well as potentially prompt them to act for change—whether that is within themselves, their family and friends, or having an impact on a larger community.

How do you consider issues of social justice in your novels? Could you discuss some examples of this in relation to your use of craft elements?

ABTAHI: Even though my books are for younger readers, racism and microaggressions are a big part of them. In *Perfectly Parvin*, fourteen-year-old Parvin struggles incredibly hard with Western beauty norms and the devaluing of her Persian culture. In *Azar on Fire* she experiences difficulties due to her throat condition. When I think of a character, I truly have to inhabit them. In my craft elements I encourage authors to think about both the good and the difficult that the protagonist's body can come with throughout the story.

JONES: The injustices, violence, and social trauma that exists in the real world and adult literature does and should exist in YA novels. I've written about sexual assault and jailed parents in my first novel and racism and alcoholism in my second. The third novel focused on untreated mental illness—depression and suicide specifically. The fourth looked at grief. The manuscript my agent is currently shopping looks at domestic violence and its aftermath. I try to look at these issues through the lens of a child or teen—to examine how these societal issues shape their world.

VEGA: Social justice is something that I am currently exploring in a few books I'm writing—two novels and a picture book. My novels usually start with character, so when I consider social justice issues, it starts with how the issue is affecting or will affect the characters. If it's not something my character is experiencing, do they have any point of reference to understand the situation or will they be on a "learning/awareness" journey? How will this situation disrupt their life and force them to view their life, themselves, or someone else differently? What mistakes will they make that they will need to own in order to grow? Who might they lose in the process?

I am also working on a few picture books that deal with social justice issues. One is how a community comes together to help support each other after they experience an "affront." In this story, I'm focused a lot on the theme of community and looking at how language and rhythm can invite the reader/listener into the experience, becoming part of the community represented in the story.

When you weave social justice themes into your storytelling, how do you think this impacts your readers, especially younger readers? What kind of feedback do you hear from them on these topics?

JONES: The book I'm co-writing with Denise Vega has social justice at the core of the plot. Our book will focus on two high school juniors who witness a sexual assault at a school event. They are dismayed by the school's lack of procedure to handle sexual assault. They band together to create an app to help their fellow students feel safe. After seeing how my daughter's high school handled a similar situation, Denise and I created a "ripped from headlines" plot to explore how the #metoo movement has empowered this generation to speak out and act when they see injustice.

VEGA: I've become more committed to social justice issues in my writing within the last few years so I can't speak to feedback from my readers. I look forward to interesting discussion with them in the future!

Representation is a hot topic in writers' circles these days. Writers and readers are asking, "Who should be represented, and by whom?" and discussing what happens when that representation goes awry and why. Could you speak a little to your thoughts on representation and why the nuances of representation matter?

ABTAHI: Representation absolutely matters, though I think there is room for folks who write outside their exact experience. To this day I get letters from readers saying how badly they wished they'd had Parvin and Azar in their childhoods. Because I wrote about my experience, I was able to access the tuning fork of my soul, and that vibration resonates with a lot more people.

JONES: My worry is that the publishing industry will think that white authors including characters in their novels that are people of color or LGBTQIA+ equals representation. As a member of the Society of Children's Book Writers and Illustrators (SCWBI), I'm allowed to vote for the award they give out each year, and each year I see books that feature POC on the covers, but the author is white.

POC and LGBTQIA+ authors are uniquely qualified to write POC and LGBTQIA+ characters, bringing authentic experiences and frames of reference to the story. As of 2019, the publishing industry was overwhelmingly white, straight, female, and nondisabled. In 2001, most of the books that were about POC of color were written by white authors. True representation is when POC and LGBTQIA+ characters are written by POC and LGBTQIA+ authors. AND that get published and marketed in numbers representing their population percentage.

VEGA: I recently spoke to some high school classes who were working on their own picture books. We talked about diversity, representation in books, and the importance of *their* voices and *their* experiences in stories. As I walked around the class and looked at some of the projects and asked questions, I saw how each creator was seeing a situation through their own unique lens, making the story *theirs*. Nuance in representation matters because of that uniqueness, demonstrating what makes each person beautiful, giving readers a window into a fully realized being who is not just one thing, not just a stock character that's supposed to represent a particular group or community. And yet, along with those nuances and that uniqueness, we connect with universal truths and human experiences found in nearly every story. We nod in agreement or recognition, even as we may experience something new through the lens of that creator.

What is your hope for the future of YA fiction writing and publishing?

ABTAHI: I hope that book bans become a thing of the past, first off. But more than that, I hope that publishing gives more chances to mid and backlist authors and not just the next shiny new acquisition, something that plagues YA especially. There's such an incredible crop of new authors and I hope they get their moment to shine.

JONES: I hope the industry keeps attempting to correct its past lack of diversity. I hope it maintains the high writing quality that has historically existed in the genre.

VEGA: I hope we will continue to see many more voices represented—from gender expression to physical, emotional and neurodiversity, appearance, location, and the intersectionality of the many attributes that make teens complex and beautiful beings. There are few restrictions on young adult literature and I'd love to see it continue to reflect the reality of the lives of young people with respect, love, and humor where appropriate.

How can we use the power of storytelling to keep up the momentum of social activism and continue to inspire the younger generations?

JONES: One of the most powerful aspects of reading is the ability to see and feel things through the eyes of a character whose life experience is vastly different than yours. Second to traveling the world, reading has the powerful effect of opening the eyes and minds of people to the struggle of different cultures and races. Once we reach them through books, encouraging them to take steps in real life is a smaller leap.

VEGA: I believe we, as humans, *are* story, which is why we connect so deeply with stories that resonate with us. Stories can change lives, and we must remain committed to writing about these topics—as both the main theme or plot of a story as well as a backdrop or subplot. We need to be committed to diving into social justice issues and the emotions around them and be unafraid to address those issues, even if they make us or others uncomfortable. It is that discomfort that makes for impactful stories that can change perspectives and inspire action.

QUESTIONS for READERS

Our final anthology section on "Futures" is all about reflection and questioning. As such, we wanted to provide a space for readers to give voice to your own thoughts and experiences in relation to social justice and to re-imagining the future.

What would you like to give voice to?

How does reading and/or writing help you get through "the dark times"?

How do you survive and thrive when everything feels like it is on fire?

What bodily and/or place-based experiences have you had that overlap or resonate with the pieces in this book?

What is your hope for a re-imagining of our societal and cultural future?

What actions would help us move individually and/or collectively
toward that re-imagined future?

CONTRIBUTORS

Growing up in the DC area, OLIVIA ABTAHI devoured books and hid in empty classrooms during school to finish them. Her debut novel, *Perfectly Parvin*, was published in 2021 by Penguin Random House Putnam Books For Young Readers, receiving the SCBWI Golden Kite Honor, a YALSA Odyssey  Honor, and numerous starred reviews. Her sophomore novel, *Azar on Fire*, was published in August 2022, and her middle grade debut, *Twin Flames*, comes out in 2024. She currently lives in Denver, Colorado, with her husband and daughter.

R. ALAN BROOKS teaches graphic novel writing for Regis University's MFA program and Lighthouse Writers Workshop. He's the author of *The Burning Metronome* and *Anguish Garden*, graphic novels featuring social commentary. His award-winning weekly comic for *The Colorado Sun*, "What'd I  Miss?" has been praised for its direct engagement with social issues. His TED Talk on the importance of art reached 1 million views in 2 months. His graphic novel work is featured in the Denver Art Museum's renovated Western exhibit. He hosts the Denver Museum of Contemporary Art's "How Art Is Born" podcast, as well as his own "MotherF★★ker In A Cape" comics podcast, and has written comic books for Image Comics, Zenescope Entertainment, Pop Culture Classroom, and more.

STEVEN DUNN is the author of two novels from Tarpaulin Sky Press: *Potted Meat* (2016) and *water & power* (2018). His co-authored novel with Katie Jean Shinkle, *Tannery Bay*, is forthcoming from FC2/  University of Alabama Press in Spring 2024.

CAROLINA EBEID is a multimedia poet and author of *You Ask Me to Talk About the Interior* and the chapbook *Dauerwunder: a brief record of facts*. Her work has been supported by the Stadler Center for Poetry at Bucknell University, Bread Loaf, CantoMundo, a National Endowment for the Arts fellowship, as well as a residency fellowship from the Lannan Foundation. A longtime editor, she helps edit poetry at *The Rumpus* as well as the online zine *Visible Binary*. She teaches at the Mile-High MFA program at Regis University and Lighthouse Writers Workshop.

STEVEN COLE HUGHES is a scriptwriting mentor at Regis University's Mile-High MFA, and assistant professor and director of theatre at Western Colorado University. His full-length plays include: *Indiana*, *The Bad Man*, *Billy Hell*, *Slabtown*, *cowboyily*, *Arabia*, *Battleground State*, *Dogs by Seven*, and *Poor Devils*. His plays for young audiences are: *The Presidents!*, *The Wright Stuff*, and *The Geography of Adventure*. His plays have been produced by the Bloomington Playwrights Project, the Coterie Theatre, Creede Repertory Theatre, Curious Theatre Company, Denver Center for the Performing Arts, and Western Colorado University. He is the winner of the Denver Post Ovation Award for Best New Work for *Billy Hell*, and the Ovation Award for Special Achievement for *The Billy Trilogy*. He has a BA in theatre from Indiana University and an MFA from the National Theatre Conservatory.

KRISTEN IVERSEN'S books include the award-winning *Full Body Burden: Growing Up in the Nuclear Shadow of Rocky Flats* (Crown/Random House, now a forthcoming documentary); *Molly Brown: Unraveling the Myth*; *Shadow Boxing: Art and Craft in Creative Nonfiction*; the anthologies *Doom with a View:*

Historical and Cultural Contexts of the Rocky Flats Nuclear Weapons Plant and *Don't Look Now: Things We Wish We Hadn't Seen*; and a forthcoming literary biography, *Friend and Faithful Stranger: Nikola Tesla in the Gilded Age.* A collection of new and published essays, *Wide and Generous World*, is also forthcoming. Her work has appeared in the *New York Times, American Scholar, The Nation, Fourth Genre*, and others, and she has lectured widely across the US and abroad. Iversen is professor of English/Creative Writing at the University of Cincinnati and Literary Nonfiction Editor of the *Cincinnati Review*. She holds a PhD from the University of Denver.

TRACI L. JONES was raised in Denver, Colorado. She has a BA in Psychology from Pomona College and a MS in Advertising from the University of Denver. Her debut novel, *Standing Against the Wind*, was published by Farrar, Straus and Giroux (FSG) in 2006 and won the Coretta Scott King/ John Steptoe New Talent Award in 2007. FSG would also publish *Finding My Place* (2010) and *Silhouetted by the Blue* (2011). In 2018 she signed with Metamorphosis Literary Agency. Her fourth book, *Ransoming the Captive*, was published by Black Rose Writing in 2022. In 2016, Jones joined the Mile-High MFA in Creative Writing program at Regis University in Denver, Colorado, where she teaches young adult fiction. In the summer of 2020, she joined Lighthouse Writers Workshop as a YA instructor. She also teaches a YA literature and pop culture class for the University of Colorado at Denver Honors Program.

TARASHEA NESBIT'S second novel, *Beheld*, was a *Publishers Weekly* Best Fiction Book of the Year and a *New York Times* Notable Book of the Year, among other accolades. Her first novel, *The Wives of Los Alamos*, was a finalist for the PEN/Robert

W. Bingham Prize. Her essays have been featured in the *New York Times*, *Granta*, *Literary Hub*, *The Guardian*, and elsewhere.

LORI OSTLUND'S first book, *The Bigness of the World*, won the 2008 Flannery O'Connor Award for Short Fiction, the California Book Award for First Fiction, and the Edmund White Debut Fiction Award. Her second book, *After the Parade*, was a Barnes & Noble Discover pick, a *New York Times* Editors' Choice, and a finalist for the Center for Fiction First Novel Prize. Her work has appeared in *Best American Short Stories* and the *PEN/O. Henry Prize Stories* as well as in journals such as *New England Review* and *ZYZZYVA*. Lori received a Rona Jaffe Foundation Award and was a 2017 Joyce Carol Oates Prize finalist. She is on the Mile-High MFA faculty at Regis University and is the series editor of the Flannery O'Connor Award for Short Fiction. She lives in San Francisco—in a very small house—with her wife, the novelist Anne Raeff, their daughter Juztice, and two cats.

KHADIJAH QUEEN is the author of six books of innovative poetry and hybrid prose, most recently *Anodyne* (Tin House 2020), winner of the William Carlos Williams award from the Poetry Society of America. A zuihitsu about the pandemic, "False Dawn," appeared in *Harper's Magazine* and was selected as a Notable Essay by Best American in 2020. Her verse play *Non-Sequitur* (Litmus Press) won the Leslie Scalapino Award for Innovative Women's Performance Writing, which included a full staged production at Theaterlab NYC in 2015. Individual poems and prose appear in *American Poetry Review, Fence, Poets & Writers Magazine*, the *New York Times, The Poetry Review* (UK) and widely elsewhere. A Cave Canem alum, she holds a PhD in English and Literary Arts from University of Denver.

JENNY SHANK'S story collection *Mixed Company* won
the George Garrett Fiction prize and the Colorado
Book Award in General Fiction, and her novel *The
Ringer* won the High Plains Book Award and was a
finalist for the Reading the West Award. Her stories,
essays, satire, and book reviews have appeared
in *The Atlantic, The Washington Post, The Guardian, Los Angeles Times,
Prairie Schooner, Alaska Quarterly Review, The Toast, Barrelhouse, The
McSweeney's Book of Politics and Musicals, Dear McSweeney's,* and *Love
in the Time of Time's Up.* Her work has been honorably mentioned
by *The Best American Essays,* the *Pushcart Prize* anthology, and her
mother. She is a longtime book critic, member of the National Book
Critics Circle, and participant on the NBCC John Leonard Prize
committee for best first book. She teaches in the Mile-High MFA
program at Regis University and the Lighthouse Writers Workshop
in Denver.

SUZI Q. SMITH is an award-winning artist, organizer,
and educator who lives in Denver, Colorado. She has
created, curated, coached, and taught in Denver for
over 20 years, managing the largest poetry festivals
that Denver has seen to date. In addition to being
a TEDx speaker in Denver and Boulder, Suzi has
performed throughout the United States for over a decade, and has
shared stages with Nikki Giovanni, the late Gil Scott Heron, and
many more. The author of poetry collections *Poems for the End
of the World, A Gospel of Bones,* and *Thirteen Descansos,* Suzi is also
a singer-songwriter, playwright, and multi-disciplinary creative.
Currently, she is affiliate faculty with Regis University's Mile-High
MFA, Lighthouse Writers Workshop, and DU's Prison Arts Initiative,
as well as the [margins.] Conference Director for The Word. She
also serves as a community representative on the Denver County
Cultural Council.

CHRISTINE SNEED is the author of three novels, *Please Be Advised: A Novel in Memos, Little Known Facts,* and *Paris, He Said,* as well as the story collections *Portraits of a Few of the People I've Made Cry, The Virginity of Famous Men,* and *Direct Sunlight.* She is the editor of the short fiction anthology *Love in the Time of Time's Up,* and is the recipient of the Chicago Public Library Foundation's 21st Century Award, the Chicago Writers Association Book of the Year Award, *Ploughshares'* Zacharis Prize, the Grace Paley Prize in Short Fiction, among other honors. Her stories and essays have appeared in *The Best American Short Stories* and *O. Henry Prize Stories* anthologies, *The New York Times, Chicago Tribune, New England Review, The Southern Review, Ploughshares, ZYZZYVA, Boulevard, Story,* and numerous other publications. She lives in Pasadena, California.

MATHANGI SUBRAMANIAN is an award-winning writer and educator. Her novel *A People's History of Heaven* was a finalist for the Lambda Literary Award and was longlisted for the PEN/Faulkner Award and the Center for Fiction First Novel Prize, among others. Her middle grade book, *Dear Mrs. Naidu,* won the South Asia Book Award. Her shorter work has appeared in *The Washington Post, Harper's Bazaar, ms.com, The San Francisco Chronicle, Kweli Journal,* and *McSweeny's Internet Tendency,* among others. She is currently faculty at Regis University's Mile-High MFA Program and The Writer's Center, and is a guest artist at Denver School of the Arts. A Fulbright-Nehru Senior scholar and a former assistant vice president at Sesame Workshop, senior policy analyst for the New York City Council, and public school teacher in Texas and New York City, she holds a doctorate in communication and education from Columbia Teachers College.

ADDIE TSAI (any/all) is a queer nonbinary artist and writer of color who teaches creative writing at William & Mary. They also teach in Goddard College's MFA Program in Interdisciplinary Arts and Regis University's Mile-High MFA Program in Creative Writing.  Addie collaborated with Dominic Walsh Dance Theater on *Victor Frankenstein* and *Camille Claudel*, among others. They earned an MFA from Warren Wilson College and a PhD in Dance from Texas Woman's University. Addie is the author of *Dear Twin* and *Unwieldy Creatures*. She is the Fiction co-editor and editor of Features & Reviews at *Anomaly*, contributing writer at *Spectrum South*, and founding editor & editor in chief at *just femme & dandy*.

DENISE VEGA is the award-winning author of seven books for kids from toddler to teen, including the YA novel *Rock On* and the award-winning picture book *If Your Monster Won't Go to Bed*. She has also published poems, articles, and activities in a variety of publications.  In her role as a mentor for the Regis University Mile-High MFA in Creative Writing, she works with writers of young adult literature, some general fiction and facilitates a children's picture book semester. She is a member of several writing and literature organizations and lives in Denver with her family.

RACHEL WEAVER is the author of the novel *Point of Direction*, which *Oprah Magazine* named a Top Ten Book to Pick Up Now. *Point of Direction* was chosen by the American Booksellers Association as a Top Ten Debut for Spring 2014 and won the 2015 Willa Cather Award for Fiction.  She is on faculty at Regis University's low residency MFA program and at Lighthouse Writers Workshop, where she won the Beacon Award for Teaching

Excellence in 2018. Her work has appeared in *The Sun*, *Gettysburg Review*, *Blue Mesa Review*, *River Teeth*, *Alaska Women Speak*, and *Fly Fishing New England*.

DAVID HESKA WANBLI WEIDEN, an enrolled citizen of the Sicangu Lakota Nation, is the author of *Winter Counts* (Ecco 2020), nominated for an Edgar Award and winner of the Anthony, Thriller, Lefty, Barry, Macavity, Spur, High Plains, Electa Quinney, Tillie Olsen, CrimeFest (UK), and Crime Fiction Lover (UK) Awards. The novel was a *New York Times* Editors' Choice, an Indie Next pick, main selection of the Book of the Month Club, and named a Best Book of the year by NPR, *Publishers Weekly*, *Library Journal*, *The Guardian*, and other magazines. He has short stories appearing in the anthologies *Best American Mystery and Suspense Stories 2022*, *Denver Noir*, *Midnight Hour*, *This Time for Sure*, *Never Whistle at Night*, and *The Perfect Crime*. Weiden received the PEN/America Writing for Justice Fellowship and is the recipient of fellowships and residencies from MacDowell, Ucross, Ragdale, Vermont Studio Center, Sewanee, and Tin House.

ERIKA T. WURTH'S novel *White Horse* is a *New York Times* Editors' Pick, a *Good Morning America* Buzz Pick, and an Indie Next, Target Book of the Month, and Book of the Month Pick. She is both a Kenyon and Sewanee fellow, has published in *The Kenyon Review*, *Buzzfeed*, and *The Writer's Chronicle*, and is a narrative artist for the Meow Wolf Denver installation. She is an urban Native of Apache/Chickasaw/Cherokee descent. She is represented by Rebecca Friedman for books and Dana Spector for film. She lives in Denver with her partner, step-kids, and two incredibly fluffy dogs.

EDITOR

ANDREA REXILIUS is the author of *Sister Urn*
(Sidebrow, 2019), *New Organism: Essais* (Letter
Machine, 2014), *Half of What They Carried Flew
Away* (Letter Machine, 2012), and *To Be Human Is
To Be A Conversation* (Rescue Press, 2011), as well as
the chapbooks, *Séance* (Coconut Books, 2014), *To
Be Human* (Horseless Press, 2010), and *Afterworld* (above/ground
press, 2020). She earned an MFA in Poetry from the School of the
Art Institute of Chicago (2005), and a PhD in Literature & Creative
Writing from the University of Denver (2010). Andrea is the pro-
gram director for Regis University's Mile-High MFA in Creative
Writing. She also teaches in the Poetry Collective at Lighthouse
Writers Workshop in Denver, Colorado.

ACKNOWLEDGMENTS

Thank you to the following publications for first publishing versions of works in this collection.

PART I

"Carlisle Longings," David Heska Wanbli Weiden. First published in *Shenandoah: The Washington and Lee University Review*, Vol. 69, Issue 1, Fall 2019.

"Writing as a vessel for chaos," Addie Tsai. First published by *The University of Arizona Poetry Center* 1508, May 12, 2020.

"Punctum / Metaphora," "Punctum / Image Of An Intifada," "Palestine, The Metaphor," "Punctum / The Transom," and "Punctum / Sawing A Woman in Half," Carolina Ebeid. First published in *You Ask Me To Talk About the Interior*, Noemi Press 2016.

PART II

"When Death Came to Golden," Kristen Iversen. First published in *The American Scholar*, March 5, 2018.

"The Bus Driver," Lori Ostlund. First published in *Story* #16, Spring 2023.

"Dark Humor," Suzi Q. Smith. First published in *Poems for the End of the World*, Finishing Line Press, July 2021.

"Other People's Mistakes," Mathangi Subramanian. First published in *Kweli Journal*, May 2022.

"Candy Francois," Erika T. Wurth. First published in *Split Lip Magazine*, Nov. 14, 2013.

PART III

"In the event of an apocalypse, be ready to die," Khadijah Queen. First published in *Anodyne,* Tin House Books 2020 and in *Boston Review*, December 28, 2017.

"Hockey Forever . . . Or as Long as it Lasts," Jenny Shank. First published in *The Missouri Review*, BLAST online, summer 2020.

"Dizzy," Rachel Weaver. First published in *Sun Magazine* in July 2017.

"Sometimes the Floor Needs Swept," TaraShea Nesbit. First published in *Literary Hub*, March 18, 2020.

"The Dream Act," Khadijah Queen. First published in *Non-Sequitur,* Litmus Press, 2015.

• • •

Thank you to the Mile-High MFA in Creative Writing Program at Regis University for providing us a space to mentor students on the craft of writing. And to Heather Garbo at The Bookies Press for her dedication and guidance toward putting this anthology together. I'd also like to give a special shout out to R. Alan Brooks who helped with the initial conception of this project and who painstakingly gathered all our contributor submissions. Thank you to the faculty (the contributors) at the Mile-High MFA for making this book possible. And to HR Hegnauer for her skilled design.